SO-CFY-960

from Teddy
To
Joyce Glass

Atlanta's Treasures

∽

Recipes from
AT&T
Telephone Pioneers
of America

Atlanta

THE GATE CITY OF THE SOUTH

This cookbook is a collection of our favorite recipes,
which are not necessarily original recipes.

Published by: Century Chapter, Telephone Pioneers of America

Copyright© Century Chapter
Telephone Pioneers of America
1200 Peachtree Street
Prom I, Floc 9133
Atlanta, Georgia 30309

Library of Congress Number: 94-61515
ISBN: 0-87197-417-7

Designed, Edited and Printed by: Favorite Recipes® Press
P.O. Box 305142
Nashville, Tennessee 37230
1-800-358-0560

Manufactured in the United States of America
First Printing: 1994   7,500 copies

Dedication

This cookbook is dedicated to the thousands of volunteers who make up the AT&T Pioneer family. With the dedication, perserverance and love these Pioneers, Pioneer Partners, and Life Members display, we accomplish multitudes of projects. A special thanks to the many volunteers who helped create this cookbook by contributing their recipes and their time. Thanks to you, our Pioneers are "making the world a better place."

Acknowledgements

Committee
Cheryl Dabney, Chair
Edna Friel, Administrator

Council Representatives
Joyce Ray, Atlanta West
Barbara Fields, Azalea
Pam Cown, Cherokee
Marge Morgester, Magnolia
Linda Causey, Northeast
Bessie Marks, WE BTL/Cable
Jackie Powell, WE Region

Artwork
Graciously contributed by Terri Lee Ross and Brenda Reinhardt

Cover
Developed from an idea and sketch by Brenda Reinhardt

Foreword

The Telephone Pioneers of America is the world's largest industry-supported organization dedicated to community service. We enjoy a membership of more than 850,000 across the United States and Canada. The Pioneers are employees of AT&T, the Bell Systems, and selected telecommunications companies. Last year, the Pioneers contributed a record 31 million volunteer-service hours and raised more than $20 million to benefit those in need.

We actively support many of Atlanta's most worthwhile efforts. Some of our foremost efforts are:

Aid Atlanta	Egleston Children's Hospital
American Red Cross	Various homes for battered women
Adopt-a-Highway	and children
Brook Run	Various youth development centers
Camp Twin Lakes	Various nursing homes

Pioneers working on their own or teaming up with other service-minded organizations are involved in environmental, human services, health and education and life enrichment efforts in every corner of the United States and Canada.

Your support of our efforts through the purchase of this cookbook is sincerely appreciated.

Statement of Purpose

- To promote and participate in activities that respond to community needs and problems;
- To provide a means of friendly association for eligible telecommunications employees and those retired;
- To foster among them a continuing fellowship and a spirit of mutual helpfulness;
- To contribute to the progress of the Association and promote the happiness, well-being and usefulness of the membership;
- To exemplify and perpetuate those principles which have come to be regarded as the ideals and traditions of the industry.

Contents

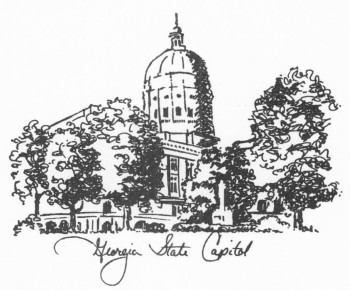

Georgia State Capitol

Contributors

Mariann R. Abbate
Gladys Ammerman
Jane Arnold
Lula Banks
Pamela S. Baustert
Jacklin Bikkovche
Bill Bingham
Helen Blackwell
Charles A. Blake
Stella R. Bledsoe
Monica Keel Blumberg
Marklyn Boucher
Crystal Bowman
Marilyn J. Bowman
Mary J. Bowman
Aneta Bowzer
Patsy Britton
C. L. Burch
Dale Burke
Ruth Burke
Patricia G. Caine
Ralph Campbell
Delois Caruthers
Nancy Cash
Faye E. Causey
Linda Causey
JoAnn Chapman
Anna Charping
Kay Closson
Pamela H. Cown
Tonya Craig
Latasha Crawford
JoAnn Cummings
Dixie Curtis
Cheryl Dabney
Debra Dagen
Jessica L. Davis
Lucille Davis
Sherry Davis
Helen L. Dover
Jean Dunlop

Gloria Edge
Phyllis Ehart
Jewel Ellison
Barbara Fields
Linda Fitch
Jack Fitzgerald
Deborah Foshee
Dessie Foster
Diane Friesen
Bula Gann
Carolyn Gann
Julia P. Gaston
Lucindy Gee
Carmen Gezik
Charles Glenn
Christy Goodman
Lula Grant
Brad Grantham
Judith Grantham
Stella P. Gray
Sylvia Green
Louis L. Greene
Dottie Gregory
Janet Haggard
Debra J. Hahn
Sharon Hall
Pam Harris
Debbie Harwell
Amalie Helbert
Norma W. Hemwall
Joan Henderson
Linda Hitchcock
Russell Hitchcock
Darlene Hogan
Helen Holmberg
Judy Holmes
Peggy Hovorka
Jean Hurley
Don Jackson
Ruby Johnson
Martha Jones

Contributors

Martha Jung
Barbara Keel
Pete Keel
Linda Kick
Peggy Konar
Marion Kuhn
Carrie M. Lampkin
Yvonne Landreth
Alice Lewis
Charlene Loth
Pat Loudermilk
Terra Mahre
Gladys Marchant
Hazel Marchant
Bessie Marks
Thomas Marks
Dianne Martin
Emilia Martinez
Louise Maxwell
Jean Maynard
Betty McAdory
June McCubbin
H. L. McLain
Bonnie McLendon
Mary Miller
Gene Mitchell
Kathy Mitchell
Mary Mobley
Clarissa Moman
Marge Morgester
Peggy Murphy
Dana Nigh
Sandra Norton
Elanor Panton
Homer W. Perry
Leona Perry
Julia Pitts
Jackie Powell
Lynn Prendergast
Jeanette Putmon
Joyce Ray

Jean Reeves
Darlene Revere
Dennis Rice
Catalina Rivero
Lynn Rivers
Eloise B. Rodgers
Judith Rogers
Carolyn Santee
Hugh Self
Jack Shepard
Malinda D. Shepard
Rob Simler
Theresa A. Siskey
Diane Slaton
Susan Sloan
Bob Smith
Larry Soloman
Dwana Spurlock
Bill Stark
Brenda St. Denis
R. Stephens
Bobbie Summerour
Rachel Thompson
Sonja Tomlin
Susan Tomlin
Randy Tudor
Bonnie Turner
Fran Van Tine
Jane M. Vaughn
Holly Vincent
Michael Vogt
David Walker
Libby Walker
Bonnie J. Ward
Ann Wedgwood
Jessie M. White
Gloria Williams
Leishman Williams
Patricia Wise
Wanda Woodall
Mary L. Wright

Nutritional Profile

The editors have attempted to present these family recipes in a form that allows approximate nutritional values to be computed. Persons with dietary or health problems or whose diets require close monitoring should not rely solely on the nutritional information provided. They should consult their physicians or a registered dietitian for specific information.

Abbreviations for Nutritional Profile

Cal — Calories
Prot — Protein
Carbo — Carbohydrates

Fiber — Dietary Fiber
T Fat — Total Fat
Chol — Cholesterol

Sod — Sodium
g — grams
mg — milligrams

Nutritional information for these recipes is computed from information derived from many sources, including materials supplied by the United States Department of Agriculture, computer databanks and journals in which the information is assumed to be in the public domain. However, many specialty items, new products and processed foods may not be available from these sources or may vary from the average values used in these profiles. More information on new and/or specific products may be obtained by reading the nutrient labels. Unless otherwise specified, the nutritional profile of these recipes is based on all measurements being level.

- **Artificial sweeteners** vary in use and strength so should be used "to taste," using the recipe ingredients as a guideline. Sweeteners using aspartame (NutraSweet and Equal) should not be used as a sweetener in recipes involving prolonged heating which reduces the sweet taste. For further information on the use of these sweeteners, refer to package information.
- **Alcoholic ingredients** have been analyzed for basic ingredients, although cooking causes the evaporation of alcohol, thus decreasing caloric content.
- **Buttermilk, sour cream** and **yogurt** are the types available commercially.
- **Cake mixes** which are prepared using package directions include 3 eggs and 1/2 cup oil.
- **Chicken**, cooked for boning and chopping, has been roasted; this method yields the lowest caloric values.
- **Cottage cheese** is cream-style with 4.2% creaming mixture. Dry curd cottage cheese has no creaming mixture.
- **Eggs** are all large. To avoid raw eggs that may carry salmonella as in eggnog or 6-week muffin batter, use an equivalent amount of commercial egg substitute.
- **Flour** is unsifted all-purpose flour.
- **Garnishes**, serving suggestions and other optional additions and variations are not included in the profile.
- **Margarine** and **butter** are regular, not whipped or presoftened.
- **Milk** is whole milk, 3.5% butterfat. Lowfat milk is 1% butterfat. Evaporated milk is whole milk with 60% of the water removed.
- **Oil** is any type of vegetable cooking oil. Shortening is hydrogenated vegetable shortening.
- **Salt** and other ingredients to taste as noted in the ingredients have not been included in the nutritional profile.
- If a choice of ingredients has been given, the nutritional profile reflects the first option. If a choice of amounts has been given, the nutritional profile reflects the greater amount.

Carving on Stone Mountain

Appetizers, Beverages, Snacks

APPLE AND RAISIN CHEESE BALL

Yield:
16 servings

Approx Per Serving:
Cal 103
Prot 2 g
Carbo 9 g
T Fat 8 g
63% Calories from Fat
Chol 16 mg
Fiber 1 g
Sod 43 mg

8 ounces cream cheese, softened
2 tablespoons confectioners' sugar
2 cups chopped apples
1/2 cup raisins
1 teaspoon apple pie seasoning
1/2 cup chopped pecans

Combine cream cheese, confectioners' sugar, apples, raisins and seasoning in bowl; mix well. Shape into a ball. Roll in pecans. Place on serving plate. Chill until serving time. May substitute 1 teaspoon cinnamon for apple pie seasoning.

CONFETTI CHEESE BALLS

Yield:
32 servings

Approx Per Serving:
Cal 83
Prot 2 g
Carbo 1 g
T Fat 8 g
83% Calories from Fat
Chol 24 mg
Fiber <1 g
Sod 170 mg

24 ounces cream cheese, softened
1 (2-ounce) jar chopped pimento, drained
1 (4-ounce) jar mushrooms, drained, chopped
1 (4-ounce) can chopped black olives
1 (2-ounce) jar dried beef, chopped
4 green onions, including some tops, chopped

Combine cream cheese, pimento, mushrooms, black olives, beef and green onions in bowl; mix well. Shape into 2 large balls. May coat with pecans before serving. For a Super Bowl party, roll entire recipe into the shape of a football, coating with pecans and using pimento strips to resemble lacing.

(Previous illustration) The carving on Stone Mountain is the world's largest relief sculpture. It portrays three great leaders of the Confederacy—President Jefferson Davis, General Robert E. Lee and General Thomas J. (Stonewall) Jackson. General Lee's likeness is 138 feet tall, his sword, 58 feet long and four feet wide.

PINEAPPLE CREAM CHEESE BALL

Yield:
16 servings

Approx Per Serving:
Cal 135
Prot 3 g
Carbo 4 g
T Fat 12 g
80% Calories from Fat
Chol 31 mg
Fiber <1 g
Sod 84 mg

16 ounces cream cheese, softened
1 (8-ounce) can juice-pack crushed pineapple, drained
1 medium onion, finely chopped
Cayenne pepper to taste
1/2 cup finely chopped pecans

Combine cream cheese, pineapple, onion and pepper in bowl; mix well. Chill until firm. Shape into a ball. Roll in pecans. Place on serving dish. May add 2 tablespoons pineapple juice to mixture before chilling to use as a dip.

CHEESE RING

Yield:
16 servings

Approx Per Serving:
Cal 298
Prot 8 g
Carbo 12 g
T Fat 26 g
75% Calories from Fat
Chol 38 mg
Fiber 1 g
Sod 260 mg

16 ounces medium or sharp Cheddar cheese, shredded
1 cup mayonnaise
1 small onion, finely chopped
1 cup chopped pecans
Salt and pepper to taste
1 (8-ounce) jar strawberry preserves

Combine cheese, mayonnaise, onion, pecans, salt and pepper in bowl; mix well. Spoon into decorative ring mold. Chill until firm. Unmold onto serving plate. Serve with preserves and crackers.

HOT ARTICHOKE DIP

Yield:
16 servings

Approx Per Serving:
Cal 143
Prot 4 g
Carbo 4 g
T Fat 13 g
79% Calories from Fat
Chol 13 mg
Fiber <1 g
Sod 380 mg

2 (16-ounce) cans artichoke hearts
1 cup mayonnaise
1 cup grated Parmesan cheese
2 tablespoons lemon juice
Tabasco sauce to taste
Garlic powder to taste
Paprika to taste

Combine artichoke hearts, mayonnaise, Parmesan cheese, lemon juice, Tabasco sauce, garlic powder and paprika in bowl; mix well. Spoon into baking dish. Bake at 300 degrees for 15 minutes. Serve with Triscuit crackers.

MEX CHEESE DIP

Yield:
36 servings

Approx Per Serving:
Cal 151
Prot 10 g
Carbo 1 g
T Fat 12 g
70% Calories from Fat
Chol 39 mg
Fiber <1 g
Sod 410 mg

1 pound ground beef
1 pound hot sausage
16 ounces shredded Cheddar cheese
16 ounces hot Mexican Velveeta cheese, cut into cubes
1 (4-ounce) can chopped green chilies
1 (16-ounce) can stewed tomatoes, drained

Brown ground beef and sausage in skillet, stirring until ground beef is crumbly; drain. Combine with cheeses, green chilies and tomatoes in large bowl; mix well. Spoon into slow cooker. Simmer, covered, on Low until cheese melts, stirring occasionally. Serve with tortilla chips.

CHILI CON QUESO

Yield:
24 servings

Approx Per Serving:
Cal 163
Prot 12 g
Carbo 6 g
T Fat 10 g
56% Calories from Fat
Chol 39 mg
Fiber 2 g
Sod 560 mg

1¹/₂ pounds ground beef
1 (15-ounce) can refried beans
1 (4-ounce) can chopped green chilies
1 (15-ounce) can tomato sauce with tomato bits
3 tablespoons taco sauce
16 ounces Velveeta cheese, cut into cubes
1 (15-ounce) can tomatoes, drained, diced
1 tablespoon instant onion

Brown ground beef in skillet, stirring until crumbly; drain. Combine with beans, green chilies, tomato sauce, taco sauce, cheese, tomatoes and instant onion in bowl; mix well. Spoon into 2-quart slow cooker. Cook on Low until heated through.

COLD CHILI

Yield:
4 servings

Approx Per Serving:
Cal 59
Prot 2 g
Carbo 13 g
T Fat 1 g
10% Calories from Fat
Chol 0 mg
Fiber 4 g
Sod 16 mg

1 clove of garlic, chopped
Salt to taste
3 green tomatoes, chopped
1 red tomato, chopped
6 to 8 fresh jalapeño peppers, chopped
1 large onion, chopped

Combine garlic, salt, tomatoes, peppers and onion in bowl; mix well. Chill, covered, until serving time.

Lullwater House - Emory

HOT CRAB DIP

Yield:
16 servings

Approx Per
Serving:
Cal 106
Prot 6 g
Carbo 1 g
T Fat 9 g
73% Calories
from Fat
Chol 63 mg
Fiber <1 g
Sod 161 mg

8 ounces cream cheese,
  softened
2 (6-ounce) cans crab
  meat, drained
2 hard-boiled eggs,
  finely chopped
1 clove of garlic, finely
  chopped

1 teaspoon onion juice
1 teaspoon prepared
  mustard
1 teaspoon confectioners'
  sugar
1/8 teaspoon salt
1/4 cup mayonnaise

Combine cream cheese, crab meat, eggs, garlic, onion
juice, mustard, confectioners' sugar, salt and mayonnaise
in glass dish; mix well. Microwave until heated through.
Serve warm with crackers.

POOR MAN'S CRAB DIP

Yield:
8 servings

Approx Per
Serving:
Cal 215
Prot 1 g
Carbo 4 g
T Fat 22 g
90% Calories
from Fat
Chol 16 mg
Fiber <1 g
Sod 402 mg

1 (16-ounce) can
  artichoke hearts,
  drained, chopped
1/2 envelope Italian salad
  dressing mix

1/4 cup chopped green
  onions
1 cup mayonnaise

Combine artichokes, salad dressing mix, green onions
and mayonnaise in bowl; mix well. Spoon into serving
dish. Chill until serving time.

DEB'S NORTHERN RECIPE

Yield:
16 servings

Approx Per Serving:
Cal 300
Prot 8 g
Carbo 3 g
T Fat 29 g
85% Calories from Fat
Chol 42 mg
Fiber <1 g
Sod 377 mg

2 (2-ounce) packages corned beef
1 onion, chopped
12 ounces Swiss cheese, shredded
1 (8-ounce) can sauerkraut, drained
2 cups mayonnaise

Combine corned beef, onion, cheese, sauerkraut and mayonnaise in bowl; mix well. Spoon into quiche pan. Bake at 325 degrees for 1 hour. Serve on party rye bread or crackers.

PIZZA DIP

Yield:
8 servings

Approx Per Serving:
Cal 224
Prot 10 g
Carbo 13 g
T Fat 16 g
61% Calories from Fat
Chol 68 mg
Fiber 2 g
Sod 620 mg

8 ounces cream cheese, softened
1 cup catsup
1 (4-ounce) can shrimp, chopped
1 tablespoon horseradish
5 green onions, chopped
1 cup peeled seeded chopped tomatoes
$1/2$ cup black olives, chopped
1 cup chopped green bell pepper
1 cup shredded Monterey Jack cheese

Spread cream cheese in shallow serving dish. Combine catsup, shrimp and horseradish in bowl; mix well. Spread over cream cheese. Layer green onions, tomatoes, black olives, green pepper and cheese over top. Chill until serving time. Serve with crackers or tortilla chips.

SPINACH DIP

Yield:
12 servings

**Approx Per
Serving:**
*Cal 220
Prot 2 g
Carbo 7 g
T Fat 21 g
83% Calories
from Fat
Chol 24 mg
Fiber 1 g
Sod 355 mg*

1 (10-ounce) package
chopped spinach,
thawed
1¹/₂ cups sour cream
1 cup mayonnaise

1 envelope vegetable
soup mix
3 green onions, chopped
1 (8-ounce) can water
chestnuts, chopped

Drain spinach, pressing out all liquid. Combine with sour cream, mayonnaise and soup mix in bowl; mix well. Stir in green onions and water chestnuts. Spoon into serving dish. Chill for 2 hours.

MEXICAN DIP

Yield:
12 servings

**Approx Per
Serving:**
*Cal 156
Prot 2 g
Carbo 5 g
T Fat 15 g
83% Calories
from Fat
Chol 18 mg
Fiber 1 g
Sod 118 mg*

2 cups sour cream
2 tablespoons
mayonnaise
1 envelope Italian salad
dressing mix

Salt and pepper to taste
Tabasco sauce to taste
2 medium avocados,
diced
1 medium tomato, diced

Mix sour cream and mayonnaise in bowl. Add salad dressing mix, salt, pepper and Tabasco sauce; mix well. Stir in avocados and tomato. Spoon into serving dish. Serve with tortilla chips.

SEAFOOD MOUSSE

Yield:
16 servings

Approx Per Serving:
Cal 194
Prot 7 g
Carbo 4 g
T Fat 17 g
78% Calories from Fat
Chol 65 mg
Fiber <1 g
Sod 416 mg

2 envelopes unflavored gelatin
1/2 cup hot water
1 (10-ounce) can tomato soup
8 ounces cream cheese, softened
1 cup mayonnaise

8 to 12 ounces chopped cooked shrimp
1/2 cup chopped celery
1/2 cup chopped onion
1/2 cup chopped stuffed green olives
1/4 cup chopped parsley

Soften gelatin in a small amount of cold water in bowl. Add hot water, stirring until gelatin dissolves. Stir in soup. Blend cream cheese and mayonnaise in small bowl. Stir into soup mixture with shrimp, celery, onion, green olives and parsley. Spoon into mold. Chill until set. Unmold onto serving dish.

HOT CRAB SALAD CANAPÉS

Yield:
4 servings

Approx Per Serving:
Cal 488
Prot 36 g
Carbo 43 g
T Fat 19 g
36% Calories from Fat
Chol 147 mg
Fiber 4 g
Sod 1746 mg

4 English muffins, cut into halves
1 (10-ounce) can cream of mushroom soup
1/3 cup milk
1 small onion, chopped
3 cups chopped celery
1/4 teaspoon seafood seasoning
1 pound crab meat

1 1/2 tablespoons butter
1 1/2 tablespoons flour
1/4 teaspoon Worcestershire sauce
1/2 teaspoon salt
Pepper to taste
3/4 cup milk
1/2 cup shredded Swiss cheese

Toast English muffins. Combine soup, 1/3 cup milk, onion, celery and seafood seasoning in saucepan. Cook over low heat for 10 minutes, stirring often. Add crab meat. Cook until heated through, stirring gently. Melt butter in heavy saucepan. Remove from heat. Blend in next 4 ingredients. Stir in 3/4 cup milk gradually. Cook over low heat until thickened, stirring constantly. Cook for 5 minutes longer. Stir in cheese until melted. Place muffins on ovenproof serving plate. Top each half with crab meat mixture. Pour cheese sauce over top. Broil until cheese sauce is lightly browned. Cut into bite-sized pieces.

BOURBON FRANKS

Approx Per
Serving:
Cal 418
Prot 13 g
Carbo 11 g
T Fat 33 g
71% Calories
from Fat
Chol 57 mg
Fiber <1 g
Sod 1364 mg

4 or 5 green onions with tops, chopped
1/2 cup catsup
3/4 cup bourbon
1/2 cup packed dark brown sugar
Red pepper flakes to taste
4 (1-pound) packages cocktail wieners

Combine green onions, catsup, bourbon, brown sugar and red pepper flakes in saucepan. Cook until brown sugar dissolves, stirring constantly. Place cocktail wieners in heavy saucepan. Pour heated sauce over top. Simmer, covered, for 1 hour. Simmer, uncovered, for 30 minutes longer.

COCKTAIL MEATBALLS

Yield:
16 servings

Approx Per
Serving:
Cal 230
Prot 15 g
Carbo 23 g
T Fat 9 g
35% Calories
from Fat
Chol 69 mg
Fiber 2 g
Sod 585 mg

2 pounds ground beef
1 cup rolled oats
1/3 cup parsley flakes
2 eggs
2 tablespoons soy sauce
1/3 cup catsup
2 tablespoons minced onion
1/2 teaspoon garlic salt
1/4 teaspoon pepper
Oil for frying
1 (16-ounce) can jellied cranberry sauce
1 (12-ounce) bottle of chili sauce
2 tablespoons brown sugar
1 tablespoon lemon juice

Combine ground beef, oats, parsley, eggs, soy sauce, catsup, onion, garlic salt and pepper in bowl; mix well. Shape into small balls. Fry in hot oil in skillet until browned; drain. Mix cranberry sauce, chili sauce, brown sugar and lemon juice in saucepan. Add meatballs. Simmer, covered, for several hours. Serve hot.

Nutritional information does not include oil for frying.

FIREHOUSE MEATBALLS

Yield:
8 servings

Approx Per
Serving:
Cal 199
Prot 13 g
Carbo 17 g
T Fat 9 g
42% Calories
from Fat
Chol 89 mg
Fiber 1 g
Sod 1289 mg

3/4 pound ground beef
2 eggs, beaten
3/4 cup fine dry bread
  crumbs
1/2 teaspoon MSG
1 1/2 tablespoons minced
  onion
1/2 teaspoon prepared
  horseradish
3 drops of Tabasco sauce
3/4 teaspoon salt
1/2 teaspoon black pepper
1 tablespoon butter
3/4 cup catsup

1/2 cup water
1/4 cup cider vinegar
2 tablespoons brown
  sugar
1 tablespoon minced
  onion
2 teaspoons
  Worcestershire sauce
1 teaspoon dry mustard
3 drops of Tabasco sauce
1 1/2 teaspoons salt
1/4 teaspoon black pepper
Cayenne pepper to taste

Combine ground beef, eggs, bread crumbs, MSG, 1 1/2 tablespoons onion, horseradish, 3 drops of Tabasco sauce, 3/4 teaspoon salt and 1/2 teaspoon pepper in bowl; mix well. Shape into 3/4-inch balls. Brown in butter in skillet, turning frequently to preserve roundness; drain. Combine catsup, water, vinegar, brown sugar, 1 tablespoon onion, Worcestershire sauce, dry mustard, remaining Tabasco sauce, 1 1/2 teaspoons salt, 1/4 teaspoon black pepper and cayenne pepper in saucepan; mix well. Cook until heated through. Add browned meatballs. Simmer for 1 1/2 hours. Spoon into chafing dish at serving time. Serve with cocktail crackers.

Sausage and Cheese Balls

Combine 4 cups shredded Cheddar cheese and 1 pound hot or mild bulk sausage in a large bowl. Let cheese and sausage stand at room temperature until softened. Add 3 cups buttermilk baking mix and mix well. Shape into small balls; place on baking sheet. Bake at 400 degrees for 10 to 12 minutes or until brown; drain on paper towels. Yield: 100 sausage and cheese balls.

MEATBALLS

Yield:
16 servings

Approx Per
Serving:
Cal 191
Prot 14 g
Carbo 11 g
T Fat 9 g
41% Calories
from Fat
Chol 69 mg
Fiber <1 g
Sod 372 mg

2 pounds ground beef
1 cup corn flake crumbs
2 eggs
2 or 3 drops of soy sauce
Onion flakes to taste
Salt and pepper to taste
1 cup Burgundy wine

1 (12-ounce) bottle of
chili sauce
3 tablespoons brown
sugar
1 teaspoon oregano
2 drops of soy sauce

Combine ground beef, corn flake crumbs, eggs, 2 or 3 drops of soy sauce, onion flakes, salt and pepper in bowl; mix well. Shape by teaspoonfuls into balls. Cook in Dutch oven until browned. Mix wine, chili sauce, brown sugar, oregano and 2 drops of soy sauce in saucepan. Simmer for 20 minutes. Pour over cooked meatballs. Bake, covered, at 350 degrees for 1½ hours.

STUFFED MUSHROOMS

Yield:
8 servings

Approx Per
Serving:
Cal 257
Prot 7 g
Carbo 4 g
T Fat 24 g
82% Calories
from Fat
Chol 51 mg
Fiber 1 g
Sod 377 mg

1 pound medium
mushrooms
3 tablespoons butter
8 ounces cream cheese,
softened
1/2 cup grated Parmesan
cheese

2 tablespoons chopped
green onions
5 slices chopped cooked
bacon
4 or 5 cloves of garlic,
minced
1/4 cup margarine

Remove mushroom stems. Chop enough stems to measure 1/2 cup. Place mushroom caps stem side up in baking dish. Sauté chopped stems in butter in skillet for 5 minutes. Remove from heat. Stir in cream cheese, Parmesan cheese, green onions and bacon. Stuff mushroom caps. Sauté garlic in margarine in small skillet. Drizzle over stuffed mushroom caps. Broil until golden brown.

HOT DILL PICKLES

Yield:
16 servings

Approx Per
Serving:
Cal 28
Prot 1 g
Carbo 8 g
T Fat <1 g
4% Calories
from Fat
Chol 0 mg
Fiber 1 g
Sod 4799 mg

3 to 4 pounds small
  cucumbers
4 heads fresh dill
4 hot peppers

2 quarts water
1 quart white vinegar
3/4 cup salt

Wash cucumbers; pat dry. Place 1 head dill and 1 hot pepper in each of 4 hot sterilized 1-pint canning jars. Pack cucumbers in jars. Combine water, vinegar and salt in saucepan. Bring to a boil. Pour into filled jars, leaving 1/2-inch headspace; seal with 2-piece lids. Let stand for 30 days.

POTATO SKINS

Yield:
variable

Nutritional
information
for this
recipe is not
available.

Frozen potato wedges
Shredded mild Cheddar
  cheese

Chopped scallions
Bacon bits
Sour cream

Bake potato wedges for 10 to 15 minutes using package directions. Layer cheese, scallions and bacon bits over top. Bake for 3 to 5 minutes longer or until cheese melts. Serve with sour cream.

BARBECUE SHRIMP

Yield:
16 servings

Approx Per Serving:
Cal 122
Prot 15 g
Carbo 2 g
T Fat 6 g
43% Calories from Fat
Chol 133 mg
Fiber <1 g
Sod 239 mg

3 pounds deveined shrimp
Cajun or Creole seasoning to taste
2 onions, cut into strips
1 green bell pepper, chopped
Oregano to taste
Parsley to taste
Bay leaves to taste
5 tablespoons plus 1 teaspoon margarine
4 tablespoons Worcestershire sauce
1 teaspoon to 1 tablespoon oil-packed minced garlic
1 tablespoon olive oil

Place shrimp in baking dish. Sprinkle with Cajun seasoning. Add onions, green pepper, oregano, parsley and bay leaves. Melt margarine in saucepan. Stir in Worcestershire sauce, garlic and olive oil. Pour over shrimp. Bake at 300 degrees for 1¹/4 hours, turning every 25 minutes. Discard bay leaves.

SPINACH BALLS

Yield:
16 servings

Approx Per Serving:
Cal 168
Prot 6 g
Carbo 9 g
T Fat 12 g
63% Calories from Fat
Chol 81 mg
Fiber 1 g
Sod 386 mg

2 (10-ounce) packages frozen spinach, cooked, well drained
2 cups stuffing mix
1 cup grated Parmesan cheese
4 eggs, beaten
³/4 cup butter, softened
1 cup chopped onion
1 clove of garlic, minced
¹/2 teaspoon thyme
Salt to taste
¹/2 teaspoon pepper

Combine spinach, stuffing mix, Parmesan cheese, eggs, butter, onion, garlic, thyme, salt and pepper in bowl; mix well. Shape into walnut-sized balls. Place on baking sheet. Freeze until hard. Place frozen spinach balls on ungreased baking sheet. Bake at 350 degrees for 10 minutes or until lightly browned. May store frozen spinach balls in freezer until needed.

OYSTER CRACKER SNACK

Yield:
12 servings

Approx Per Serving:
Cal 331
Prot 4 g
Carbo 29 g
T Fat 23 g
61% Calories from Fat
Chol 0 mg
Fiber 1 g
Sod 671 mg

1 cup vegetable oil
1 envelope ranch-style salad dressing mix
$^1/_4$ teaspoon garlic powder
$^1/_4$ teaspoon lemon pepper
2 tablespoons dillweed
1 (1-pound) package oyster crackers

Mix oil, salad dressing mix, garlic powder, lemon pepper and dillweed in bowl. Place oyster crackers in large bowl. Pour seasoned oil over top; stir until well coated. Place crackers in large baking pan. Bake at 250 degrees for 10 minutes, stirring occasionally.

SPICED PECANS

Yield:
6 servings

Approx Per Serving:
Cal 272
Prot 3 g
Carbo 15 g
T Fat 24 g
76% Calories from Fat
Chol 0 mg
Fiber 2 g
Sod <1 mg

$^1/_4$ cup sugar
$^1/_4$ teaspoon cinnamon
2 tablespoons water
2 cups pecan halves

Combine sugar, cinnamon and water in skillet. Cook until sugar dissolves. Add pecans. Cook for 3 minutes longer, stirring occasionally to coat pecans with syrup. Spoon onto waxed paper. Let stand until cool.

BAILEY'S CREAM

Yield:
10 servings

Approx Per Serving:
Cal 288
Prot 6 g
Carbo 25 g
T Fat 8 g
25% Calories from Fat
Chol 107 mg
Fiber <1 g
Sod 90 mg

1³/₄ cups rum
1 (14-ounce) can sweetened condensed milk
1 cup half and half
4 eggs
2 tablespoons chocolate syrup

2 teaspoons instant coffee powder
1 teaspoon vanilla extract
¹/₂ teaspoon almond extract

Combine rum, condensed milk, half and half, eggs, chocolate syrup, coffee powder and flavorings in blender container. Process until smooth. May substitute brandy, rye whiskey, Scotch or bourbon for rum.

KAHLUA

Yield:
18 servings

Approx Per Serving:
Cal 549
Prot 1 g
Carbo 79 g
T Fat <1 g
<1% Calories from Fat
Chol 0 mg
Fiber 0 g
Sod 3 mg

4 cups boiling water
1¹/₂ cups instant coffee powder
7 cups sugar

2 fifths of 100-proof vodka
2 vanilla beans

Remove boiling water from heat source. Stir in coffee powder and sugar until dissolved. Stir in vodka and vanilla beans. Pour into 1-gallon jug; seal. Store in cool dark place for 7 weeks. Do not use decaffeinated coffee in this recipe.

LORI'S PUNCH

Yield:
60 servings

Approx Per Serving:
Cal 114
Prot <1 g
Carbo 29 g
T Fat <1 g
1% Calories from Fat
Chol 0 mg
Fiber <1 g
Sod 1 mg

4 cups sugar
6 cups water
2 (46-ounce) cans pineapple juice
1 (46-ounce) carton orange juice
3 (6-ounce) cans frozen lemonade concentrate
8 bananas, mashed
Sprite or 7-Up to taste

Combine sugar and water in saucepan. Bring to a boil. Cook until sugar dissolves. Remove from heat. Stir in pineapple juice, orange juice, lemonade concentrate and mashed bananas. Pour into heavy zip-lock freezer bags. Freeze until firm. Remove frozen mixture from freezer 1¹/₂ hours before serving time. Place in punch bowl. Add Sprite to taste.

OPEN-HOUSE PUNCH

Yield:
28 servings

Approx Per Serving:
Cal 138
Prot <1 g
Carbo 20 g
T Fat <1 g
<1% Calories from Fat
Chol 0 mg
Fiber <1 g
Sod 5 mg

1 (12-ounce) can frozen orange juice concentrate
1 (6-ounce) can frozen lemonade concentrate
1 fifth of Southern Comfort liquor
1 gallon 7-Up

Combine frozen concentrates and liquor in punch bowl. Stir until frozen juices are almost thawed. Pour in 7-Up. May float oranges slices on top.

BRANDIED TEA

Yield:
16 servings

*Approx Per
Serving:*
Cal 70
Prot <1 g
Carbo 16 g
T Fat <1 g
*<1% Calories
from Fat*
Chol 0 mg
Fiber <1 g
Sod 1 mg

8 cups boiling water
1/2 to 1 cup sugar
1/4 cup instant lemonade
powder

2 1/2 tablespoons instant
tea powder
1/4 cup peach-flavored or
apricot-flavored brandy

Combine boiling water, sugar, lemonade powder, tea powder and brandy in saucepan; mix well.

City of Decatur, Georgia
Old Courthouse on the Square 1867

HOT BUTTERED RUM

Yield:
60 servings

*Approx Per
Serving:*
Cal 267
Prot <1 g
Carbo 17 g
T Fat 7 g
*23% Calories
from Fat*
Chol 20 mg
Fiber <1 g
Sod 71 mg

2 cups butter, softened
1 (1-pound) package
dark brown sugar
1 (1-pound) package
confectioners' sugar

1 quart vanilla ice cream
1 teaspoon nutmeg
2 teaspoons cinnamon
4 quarts rum

Combine butter, brown sugar, confectioners' sugar, ice cream, nutmeg and cinnamon in large bowl; mix well. Mix 2 tablespoons ice cream mixture and 1 jigger of rum in each cup. Fill with boiling water.

Martin Luther King's birthplace ~ Auburn Avenue

∽◦∾

Soups and Salads

BROCCOLI AND ALMOND SOUP

Yield:
6 servings

Approx Per Serving:
Cal 198
Prot 8 g
Carbo 11 g
T Fat 15 g
64% Calories from Fat
Chol 21 mg
Fiber 4 g
Sod 835 mg

1/4 cup unsalted butter
1 (12-ounce) package frozen chopped onions, thawed, drained
1 (16-ounce) package frozen broccoli cuts, thawed
1/2 cup chicken stock
1/2 cup blanched almonds, lightly toasted
3 cups chicken stock
1 1/2 teaspoons coriander
1 teaspoon salt
1/2 teaspoon white pepper

Melt butter in large heavy saucepan over medium heat. Heat until butter foams. Add onions. Sauté for 3 minutes. Add broccoli and 1/2 cup chicken stock; cover. Bring to a boil; reduce heat. Simmer for 5 minutes or until broccoli is tender. Purée with almonds in food processor. Combine with 3 cups chicken stock, coriander, salt and pepper in saucepan; mix well. Cook over medium heat until heated through. Adjust seasonings.

CHEESE SOUP

Yield:
6 servings

Approx Per Serving:
Cal 228
Prot 12 g
Carbo 26 g
T Fat 9 g
36% Calories from Fat
Chol 21 mg
Fiber 2 g
Sod 1261 mg

4 cups chicken broth
1 potato, chopped
2 carrots, chopped
2 stalks celery, chopped
1 onion, chopped
1 (16-ounce) can cream-style corn
1 (8-ounce) jar Cheez Whiz

Combine chicken broth with potato, carrots, celery and onion in large saucepan. Simmer until vegetables are tender. Add corn and Cheez Whiz. Cook just until heated through; do not boil. This recipe comes from Esther Wenske, the world's champion recipe collector.

(Previous illustration) The Martin Luther King birth home is part of the Freedom Hall Complex of the Martin Luther King, Jr. Center for Nonviolent Social Change, the living memorial carrying on Dr. King's work. The location has been designated as a National Historical Site by the United States Congress in honor of Dr. King.

BEER CHEESE SOUP

Yield:
8 servings

Approx Per
Serving:
Cal 379
Prot 21 g
Carbo 19 g
T Fat 23 g
53% Calories
from Fat
Chol 73 mg
Fiber 2 g
Sod 730 mg

2¹/₂ cups beer
1 (14-ounce) can
  chicken broth
1 cup shredded carrot
1 cup thinly sliced celery
¹/₃ cup thinly sliced
  onion
1 large potato, finely
  chopped

¹/₃ cup flour
3 cups milk
16 ounces sharp
  Cheddar cheese,
  shredded
Salt and freshly ground
  pepper to taste

Combine beer and chicken broth in 3-quart saucepan. Cook over medium-high heat just until simmering, stirring constantly. Add carrot, celery, onion and potato. Simmer, covered, for 10 to 12 minutes or until vegetables are tender. Blend flour into half the milk in small bowl. Add to soup with remaining milk. Cook for 15 minutes or until thickened, stirring frequently. Add cheese gradually, stirring until melted. Season with salt and pepper. Serve in heated soup bowls. Cheating is allowed on the beer and vegetables for this soup; just use the amounts that you like. Add fresh broccoli for variation. If the soup gets too thick, thin it with a small amount of water or additional milk.

CANADIAN CHEESE SOUP

Yield:
6 servings

Approx Per
Serving:
Cal 232
Prot 12 g
Carbo 10 g
T Fat 16 g
63% Calories
from Fat
Chol 41 mg
Fiber 1 g
Sod 460 mg

¹/₂ cup finely chopped
  carrot
¹/₄ cup finely chopped
  celery
¹/₄ cup finely chopped
  onion
2 tablespoons margarine

¹/₄ cup flour
2 cups milk
1¹/₂ cups chicken broth
Paprika to taste
1¹/₂ cups shredded sharp
  Cheddar cheese

Combine carrot, celery, onion and margarine in saucepan. Cook, covered, over low heat until vegetables are tender. Stir in flour. Add milk, chicken broth and paprika. Cook until thickened, stirring constantly. Stir in cheese. Cook just until cheese melts; do not boil.

CORN SOUP

Yield:
8 servings

Approx Per
Serving:
Cal 142
Prot 11 g
Carbo 16 g
T Fat 4 g
26% Calories
from Fat
Chol 89 mg
Fiber 2 g
Sod 437 mg

1¹/₂ tablespoons flour
2 tablespoons vegetable oil
1 medium onion, chopped
1 shallot with top, chopped
1 (16-ounce) can white cream-style corn
1 (8-ounce) can tomato sauce
6 cups water
1 pound shrimp
Salt and pepper to taste
1 tablespoon chopped parsley

Brown flour in heated oil in large saucepan. Add onion and shallot. Cook for several minutes. Add corn. Cook for several minutes. Stir in tomato sauce. Cook for several minutes. Stir in water. Bring to a boil. Add shrimp; reduce heat. Stir in salt and pepper. Simmer for 45 to 60 minutes or until done to taste, stirring in parsley about 10 minutes before end of cooking time. May add 1 chopped potato 30 minutes before end of cooking time if desired.

CHILI MY WAY

Yield:
12 servings

Approx Per
Serving:
Cal 366
Prot 30 g
Carbo 24 g
T Fat 17 g
41% Calories
from Fat
Chol 84 mg
Fiber 5 g
Sod 902 mg

3 pounds ground sirloin or ground beef
2 large onions, chopped
1 (28-ounce) can light red kidney beans
2 (10-ounce) cans tomato soup
2 (12-ounce) cans tomato juice
1 cup water
3 envelopes mild chili seasoning mix
1 envelope hot chili seasoning mix
Salt to taste

Brown ground sirloin with onions in skillet over medium heat, stirring until ground sirloin is crumbly; drain. Combine beans, soup, tomato juice, water, chili seasoning mixes and salt in large saucepan. Add ground sirloin. Cook over medium-to-high heat until heated through; reduce heat. Simmer for 30 to 45 minutes or until of desired consistency. May freeze chili and reheat if desired.

LOW-FAT MEXICAN CHILI

Yield:
12 servings

Approx Per Serving:
Cal 377
Prot 24 g
Carbo 56 g
T Fat 7 g
16% Calories from Fat
Chol 36 mg
Fiber 9 g
Sod 1116 mg

1¹/₂ pounds chicken breast filets
1 medium onion, minced
1 green bell pepper, chopped
Chopped garlic to taste
1 to 2 tablespoons crushed hot red chili pepper
2 tablespoons chili powder
2 teaspoons cumin
¹/₂ teaspoon oregano
1 teaspoon dried cilantro
1 teaspoon salt
2 (16-ounce) cans dark red kidney beans
2 (16-ounce) cans whole tomatoes
1 (8-ounce) can tomato sauce
1 (16-ounce) can whole kernel corn, drained
12 large flour tortillas

Rinse chicken and pat dry. Cut into bite-sized pieces, discarding fat. Sauté in large heavy saucepan; drain. Add next 9 ingredients; mix well. Cook until onion and green pepper are tender, stirring frequently. Add undrained beans and tomatoes, tomato sauce and corn; mix well. Simmer over low heat for 45 minutes or until done to taste, stirring occasionally. Shape tortillas over inverted custard cups on baking sheet; spray with nonstick cooking spray. Bake at 375 degrees for 15 minutes or until shells are crisp. Serve chili in tortilla shells.

CLAM CHOWDER

Yield:
6 servings

Approx Per Serving:
Cal 363
Prot 23 g
Carbo 26 g
T Fat 19 g
46% Calories from Fat
Chol 94 mg
Fiber 1 g
Sod 1778 mg

2 (10-ounce) cans cream of potato soup
2 (10-ounce) cans cream of celery soup
2 soup cans milk
1 onion, minced
¹/₄ cup butter
1 or 2 (7-ounce) cans minced clams, drained
¹/₂ teaspoon pepper

Combine soups, milk, onion, butter, clams and pepper in large saucepan; mix well. Simmer for 30 minutes. May substitute 2 tablespoons dried onion for fresh onion if desired.

GAZPACHO

Yield:
6 servings

Approx Per
Serving:
Cal 41
Prot 2 g
Carbo 10 g
T Fat <1 g
6% Calories
from Fat
Chol 0 mg
Fiber 2 g
Sod 447 mg

3 cups vegetable juice
  cocktail or tomato
  juice
1 cup chopped, peeled
  seeded cucumber
1 cup chopped peeled
  tomato

1 cup chopped green
  bell pepper
1/2 cup finely chopped
  green onions
Salt and pepper to taste

Combine vegetable juice cocktail, cucumber, tomato, green pepper, green onions, salt and pepper in bowl. Chill until serving time. Top servings with sour cream. May add 2 tablespoons chopped green chilies if desired. This makes a good first course with Mexican food.

FRENCH ONION SOUP

Yield:
8 servings

Approx Per
Serving:
Cal 325
Prot 15 g
Carbo 31 g
T Fat 15 g
42% Calories
from Fat
Chol 25 mg
Fiber 2 g
Sod 1287 mg

1 1/2 pounds onions,
  thinly sliced
3 tablespoons margarine
1 tablespoon vegetable
  oil
1/4 teaspoon sugar
5 tablespoons flour
7 cups boiling beef
  bouillon

1/2 cup dry white wine
1 teaspoon salt
Pepper to taste
8 slices toasted French
  bread
2 cups shredded Swiss
  cheese

Combine onions with margarine and oil in heavy saucepan. Cook, covered, over low heat for 5 minutes. Increase heat to medium; remove cover. Stir in sugar. Cook for 10 minutes or until onions are evenly brown, stirring frequently. Sprinkle with flour. Cook for 3 minutes, stirring constantly. Remove from heat. Stir in bouillon and wine. Season with salt and pepper. Simmer, partially covered, for 30 to 40 minutes or until done to taste, skimming occasionally. Ladle into ovenproof serving bowls. Top each serving with French bread; sprinkle with cheese. Bake in very hot oven for 10 minutes or until cheese is light brown.

BAKED POTATO SOUP

Yield:
6 servings

Approx Per
Serving:
Cal 746
Prot 23 g
Carbo 51 g
T Fat 51 g
61% Calories
from Fat
Chol 141 mg
Fiber 2 g
Sod 970 mg

4 large potatoes, baked, cooled
2/3 cup flour
2/3 cup melted butter or margarine
6 cups milk
4 green onions, chopped
12 slices bacon, crisp-fried, crumbled
1 1/4 cups shredded Cheddar cheese
3/4 teaspoon salt
1/2 teaspoon pepper
1 cup sour cream

Cut potatoes into halves lengthwise. Scoop pulp into bowl. Blend flour into butter in heavy saucepan over low heat. Cook for 1 minute, stirring constantly. Add milk gradually. Cook over medium heat until thickened, stirring constantly. Add potato pulp, 2 tablespoons of the green onions, 1/2 cup of the bacon, 1 cup of the cheese, salt and pepper; mix well. Cook until heated through. Stir in sour cream and additional milk if needed for desired consistency. Sprinkle servings with remaining green onions, bacon and cheese.

POTATO AND CHEESE SOUP

Yield:
6 servings

Approx Per
Serving:
Cal 413
Prot 20 g
Carbo 29 g
T Fat 25 g
53% Calories
from Fat
Chol 72 mg
Fiber <1 g
Sod 1881 mg

1 tablespoon minced onion
5 cups water
4 chicken bouillon cubes
1 teaspoon parsley
Celery salt and seasoned salt to taste
Salt and pepper to taste
1 (32-ounce) package frozen hashed brown potatoes
16 ounces Velveeta cheese, shredded

Combine onion, water, bouillon, parsley, celery salt, seasoned salt, salt and pepper in saucepan. Bring to a boil. Add potatoes. Cook for several minutes. Stir in cheese. Cook for 10 minutes, stirring until cheese is melted. May thicken with a mixture of cornstarch and milk if desired.

CREAMY SPINACH AND CARROT SOUP

Yield:
4 servings

Approx Per
Serving:
Cal 231
Prot 8 g
Carbo 14 g
T Fat 17 g
63% Calories
from Fat
Chol 23 mg
Fiber 3 g
Sod 765 mg

1 onion, chopped
3 tablespoons margarine
2 tablespoons flour
1 cup half and half
1 (10-ounce) can
  chicken broth
1 cup shredded carrot

1 (10-ounce) package
  frozen chopped
  spinach, thawed,
  drained
1/4 teaspoon salt
1/4 teaspoon pepper
Tabasco sauce to taste

Sauté onion in margarine in saucepan until tender. Stir in flour. Cook until smooth and bubbly. Stir in half and half and chicken broth. Add carrot, spinach, salt, pepper and Tabasco sauce. Cook over low heat until heated through, stirring occasionally.

TORTILLA SOUP

Yield:
8 servings

Approx Per
Serving:
Cal 563
Prot 36 g
Carbo 28 g
T Fat 36 g
56% Calories
from Fat
Chol 89 mg
Fiber 4 g
Sod 1750 mg

2 (14-ounce) cans
  chicken broth
1 (14-ounce) can beef
  broth
1 (16-ounce) can
  chopped tomatoes
1 (4-ounce) can chopped
  green chilies
1/2 onion, chopped
1 1/2 teaspoons cumin
4 chicken breasts,
  cooked, chopped

Salt to taste
1 tablespoon (or less)
  cornstarch
1 (8-ounce) package
  tortilla chips, crushed
2 avocados, chopped
2 cups shredded Colby
  cheese
2 cups shredded
  Monterey Jack cheese

Combine chicken broth, beef broth, tomatoes, green chilies, onion and cumin in saucepan. Simmer for 20 minutes. Add chicken and salt. Simmer for 10 minutes. Stir in cornstarch. Cook until desired consistency, stirring constantly. Ladle hot soup over crushed tortilla chips and avocados in soup bowls. Top with cheeses.

HOT AND SOUR VEGETABLE SOUP

Yield:
8 servings

Approx Per Serving:
Cal 85
Prot 5 g
Carbo 10 g
T Fat 4 g
37% Calories from Fat
Chol 0 mg
Fiber 3 g
Sod 439 mg

1 medium onion, cut into halves, slivered
3 carrots, sliced thin diagonally
2 tablespoons vegetable oil
3 cloves of garlic, minced
1 tablespoon minced fresh ginger
4 cups defatted chicken broth
1 cup water
2 tablespoons soy sauce
2 cups thinly sliced mushrooms
1 bunch watercress, stemmed
8 ounces snow peas
1 cup fresh bean sprouts
1/4 cup rice wine vinegar
Sesame oil and chili oil to taste

Sauté onion and carrots in oil in heavy saucepan over medium heat for 3 minutes. Add garlic and ginger. Cook for 1 minute, stirring constantly. Stir in chicken broth, water and soy sauce. Bring to a boil; reduce heat. Simmer, partially covered, for 2 minutes. Add mushrooms and watercress. Simmer, partially covered, for 1 minute; remove from heat. Stir in snow peas and bean sprouts. Let stand, covered, for 2 minutes. Stir in vinegar, sesame oil and chili oil. Cook for 1 minute or until heated through. Adjust seasonings.

BLUEBERRY SALAD

Yield:
12 servings

Approx Per Serving:
Cal 334
Prot 5 g
Carbo 50 g
T Fat 14 g
37% Calories from Fat
Chol 29 mg
Fiber 1 g
Sod 133 mg

3 (3-ounce) packages blackberry gelatin
2 1/2 cups boiling water
1 cup cold water
1 (21-ounce) can blueberry pie filling
1 (16-ounce) can crushed pineapple
8 ounces cream cheese, softened
1 cup sour cream
1/2 cup sugar
1 teaspoon vanilla extract
1/2 cup chopped pecans

Dissolve gelatin in boiling water in bowl. Stir in cold water. Chill until partly set. Fold in pie filling and pineapple. Spoon into shallow dish. Chill until set. Combine cream cheese with sour cream, sugar and vanilla in bowl; mix well. Spread over congealed layer; sprinkle with pecans. Chill until serving time. Cut into squares to serve.

Bing Cherry Gelatin Salad

Yield:
15 servings

**Approx Per
Serving:**
Cal 250
Prot 3 g
Carbo 34 g
T Fat 12 g
42% Calories
from Fat
Chol 19 mg
Fiber 1 g
Sod 131 mg

1 (20-ounce) can pitted
Bing cherries
1 (20-ounce) can
crushed pineapple
1 (6-ounce) package
black cherry gelatin
1 (3-ounce) package
cherry or black cherry
gelatin

8 ounces cream cheese,
softened
1/2 cup light mayonnaise
1 cup chopped pecans

Drain cherries and pineapple, reserving juices. Combine reserved juices with enough water to measure 2 cups. Bring to a boil in saucepan. Stir in gelatins until dissolved. Add cherries, pineapple, cream cheese, mayonnaise and pecans; mix well. Spoon into mold or shallow dish. Chill until set. Cut into squares or unmold onto serving plate.

Cranberry and Orange Salad

Yield:
8 servings

**Approx Per
Serving:**
Cal 358
Prot 4 g
Carbo 53 g
T Fat 16 g
39% Calories
from Fat
Chol 13 mg
Fiber 3 g
Sod 100 mg

1 cup orange juice
1 (6-ounce) package
raspberry gelatin
1 (8-ounce) can crushed
pineapple, drained
1 (16-ounce) can whole
cranberry sauce

1 cup finely chopped
celery
1 cup chopped pecans
or walnuts
1 cup sour cream

Bring orange juice to a boil in saucepan. Stir in gelatin until dissolved. Let stand until cool. Stir in pineapple, cranberry sauce, celery and pecans. Spoon 1/3 of the mixture into salad mold. Chill until firm. Spread with sour cream. Spoon remaining cranberry mixture into mold over sour cream. Chill until set. Unmold onto serving plate.

ORANGE FLUFF

Yield:
12 servings

Approx Per
Serving:
Cal 274
Prot 7 g
Carbo 30 g
T Fat 16 g
49% Calories
from Fat
Chol 5 mg
Fiber 1 g
Sod 176 mg

1 (20-ounce) can
crushed pineapple,
drained
1 (15-ounce) can
mandarin oranges,
drained
1 (4-ounce) package
orange gelatin

2 cups cottage cheese,
drained
1 cup chopped pecans
12 ounces whipped
topping

Combine pineapple, oranges and gelatin in large bowl;
mix until gelatin dissolves. Fold in cottage cheese, pecans
and whipped topping. Chill, covered, for 2 hours. May
be refrigerated for 5 to 7 days. This easy salad can also
be served as a dessert.

STRAWBERRY CONGEALED SALAD

Yield:
6 servings

Approx Per
Serving:
Cal 187
Prot 9 g
Carbo 27 g
T Fat 5 g
25% Calories
from Fat
Chol 5 mg
Fiber 1 g
Sod 267 mg

1 (20-ounce) can
juice-pack crushed
pineapple
1 small package
sugar-free strawberry
gelatin

12 ounces low-fat
cottage cheese
8 ounces light whipped
topping

Heat pineapple in saucepan until bubbly. Stir in gelatin
until dissolved. Fold in cottage cheese and whipped topping. Spoon into serving dish. Chill overnight. Satisfy
the sweet tooth of someone who is weight-conscious or
who is diabetic.

CHICKEN SALAD

Yield:
6 servings

Approx Per
Serving:
Cal 240
Prot 21 g
Carbo 15 g
T Fat 12 g
44% Calories
from Fat
Chol 48 mg
Fiber 4 g
Sod 332 mg

1 pound chicken breast
  filets
1 medium zucchini
2 large tomatoes,
  chopped
1 cup thawed frozen corn
1 avocado, chopped
1/3 cup sliced green
  onions with tops

1/2 cup picante sauce
2 tablespoons vegetable
  oil
2 tablespoons chopped
  cilantro or parsley
1 tablespoon lemon juice
1/2 teaspoon cumin
1/2 teaspoon garlic salt

Rinse chicken and pat dry. Cook chicken in water to cover in saucepan until tender; drain. Cut chicken into bite-sized pieces. Cut zucchini into halves lengthwise; cut crosswise into thin slices. Combine chicken, zucchini, tomatoes, corn, avocado and green onions in salad bowl; mix gently. Combine picante sauce, oil, cilantro, lemon juice, cumin and garlic salt in small bowl; mix well. Add to chicken mixture; mix gently. Chill until serving time, stirring occasionally.

TUNA MOUSSE SALAD

Yield:
9 servings

Approx Per
Serving:
Cal 264
Prot 11 g
Carbo 2 g
T Fat 24 g
81% Calories
from Fat
Chol 139 mg
Fiber <1 g
Sod 513 mg

2 envelopes unflavored
  gelatin
1/2 cup cold water
2/3 cup boiling water
1 (7-ounce) can white
  tuna, drained, flaked
1 cup mayonnaise
5 hard-boiled eggs,
  chilled, chopped

1/2 (8-ounce) jar stuffed
  green olives, sliced
4 green onions, sliced
1/2 teaspoon tarragon
Lemon juice to taste
Salt to taste

Soften gelatin in cold water in bowl. Stir in boiling water until gelatin dissolves completely. Add tuna, mayonnaise, eggs, olives, green onions, tarragon, lemon juice and salt; mix gently. Spoon into 8x8-inch dish. Chill until set. Cut into squares to serve.

SUMMER MACARONI SALAD

Yield:
6 servings

Approx Per
Serving:
Cal 499
Prot 7 g
Carbo 45 g
T Fat 34 g
60% Calories
from Fat
Chol 11 mg
Fiber 3 g
Sod 298 mg

8 ounces uncooked
   macaroni
1 cup chopped onion
1 cup chopped celery
1/2 cup shredded carrot
1 cup chopped cucumber
Flowerets of 1 bunch
   broccoli

1/2 cup mayonnaise
1/2 cup vegetable oil
1/4 cup vinegar
1/4 cup sugar
1 envelope Italian salad
   dressing mix

Cook macaroni using package directions; drain. Combine with onion, celery, carrot, cucumber and broccoli in bowl. Combine mayonnaise, oil, vinegar, sugar and salad dressing mix in bowl; mix well. Add to macaroni mixture; mix gently. Chill until serving time.

PASTA SALAD

Yield:
12 servings

Approx Per
Serving:
Cal 338
Prot 6 g
Carbo 35 g
T Fat 20 g
53% Calories
from Fat
Chol 0 mg
Fiber 3 g
Sod 239 mg

1 envelope zesty salad
   dressing mix
1 teaspoon sugar
Garlic powder, oregano,
   salt and pepper to taste
16 ounces pasta, cooked,
   drained
1 head broccoli, chopped
1 large carrot, chopped

2 stalks celery, chopped
1 (4-ounce) can sliced
   black olives
1 medium onion,
   chopped
1 large cucumber,
   chopped
1 large tomato, chopped

Prepare salad dressing mix using peanut oil. Combine with sugar, garlic powder, oregano, salt and pepper in large bowl; mix well. Add pasta, broccoli, carrot, celery, olives, onion, cucumber and tomato; mix gently. Chill, covered, overnight.

SPAGHETTI SALAD

Yield:
12 servings

Approx Per Serving:
Cal 244
Prot 8 g
Carbo 33 g
T Fat 10 g
34% Calories from Fat
Chol 0 mg
Fiber 2 g
Sod 458 mg

16 ounces spaghetti, cooked, drained
2 medium cucumbers, chopped
2 medium tomatoes, chopped
1/2 red onion, chopped
1 medium green bell pepper, chopped
1 small bottle of salad supreme seasoning mix
Cayenne pepper to taste
1 (7-ounce) bottle of Italian salad dressing

Combine pasta, cucumbers, tomatoes, onion and green pepper in bowl. Add salad seasoning mix, cayenne pepper and salad dressing; mix well. Chill overnight. Mix well before serving.

RICE SALAD

Yield:
6 servings

Approx Per Serving:
Cal 280
Prot 5 g
Carbo 32 g
T Fat 16 g
49% Calories from Fat
Chol 7 mg
Fiber 3 g
Sod 1048 mg

1 (7-ounce) package chicken-flavored rice mix
2 (7-ounce) jars marinated artichoke hearts
1 green bell pepper, chopped
4 scallions, thinly sliced
12 pimento-stuffed olives
1/3 cup mayonnaise
3/4 teaspoon curry powder

Cook rice using package directions, omitting step of sautéing in butter. Cool to room temperature. Drain artichokes, reserving a small amount of liquid. Combine artichokes, reserved liquid, rice, green pepper, scallions, olives, mayonnaise and curry powder in bowl; mix well. Chill for several hours.

GREEN BEAN SALAD

Yield:
12 servings

Approx Per Serving:
Cal 198
Prot 3 g
Carbo 28 g
T Fat 9 g
41% Calories from Fat
Chol 0 mg
Fiber 3 g
Sod 375 mg

1 (16-ounce) can French-style green beans
1 (16-ounce) can green peas
1 (4-ounce) jar chopped pimentos
1 large green bell pepper, sliced into thin rings
6 stalks celery, sliced
2 large onions, sliced into rings
1 cup sugar
3/4 cup cider vinegar
1/2 cup vegetable oil
1 teaspoon salt

Drain beans and peas. Combine with pimentos, green pepper, celery and onions in large salad bowl. Heat sugar and vinegar in saucepan until sugar dissolves. Cool to room temperature. Add oil and salt; mix well. Add to vegetables; mix well. Marinate, covered, in refrigerator for 24 hours or longer. This wonderful refreshing summertime treat has been a favorite at family gatherings for 25 years.

POTATO SALAD

Yield:
12 servings

Approx Per Serving:
Cal 358
Prot 6 g
Carbo 51 g
T Fat 15 g
37% Calories from Fat
Chol 81 mg
Fiber 3 g
Sod 318 mg

5 pounds potatoes, cooked, peeled, chopped
4 hard-boiled eggs, chopped
3 stalks celery, chopped
1 medium onion, chopped
2 tablespoons parsley flakes
2 cups (about) mayonnaise-type salad dressing
Salt and pepper to taste

Combine potatoes, eggs, celery and onion in large bowl. Add parsley, enough salad dressing to make of desired consistency, salt and pepper; mix gently. Chill until serving time.

Mustard Potato Salad

Yield:
12 servings

Approx Per
Serving:
Cal 372
Prot 8 g
Carbo 45 g
T Fat 19 g
44% Calories
from Fat
Chol 152 mg
Fiber 3 g
Sod 197 mg

5 pounds potatoes, peeled, coarsely chopped
Salt to taste
8 hard-boiled eggs, chopped
2 tablespoons sweet pickle salad cubes
1 large Vidalia onion, chopped
2 stalks celery, chopped
1 tablespoon mustard
1 tablespoon white vinegar
1 tablespoon sugar
3/4 to 1 cup mayonnaise

Cook potatoes in salted boiling water in saucepan for 10 to 12 minutes or until tender; drain. Combine with eggs, pickles, onion and celery in large bowl. Add mustard, vinegar, sugar, mayonnaise and salt; mix gently. Chill for 1 hour.

Marinated Vegetable Salad

Yield:
8 servings

Approx Per
Serving:
Cal 332
Prot 5 g
Carbo 50 g
T Fat 15 g
37% Calories
from Fat
Chol 0 mg
Fiber 5 g
Sod 743 mg

1 (17-ounce) can green peas, drained
1 (17-ounce) can white Shoe Peg corn, drained
1 (16-ounce) can French-style green beans, drained
1/2 cup chopped celery
1/2 to 1 cup chopped green bell pepper
1/2 cup chopped onion
1 (2-ounce) jar chopped pimento, drained
3/4 cup vinegar
1/2 cup vegetable oil
1 cup sugar
1 teaspoon salt
1/2 teaspoon pepper

Combine peas, corn, green beans, celery, green pepper, onion and pimento in large bowl; toss lightly to mix. Combine vinegar, oil, sugar, salt and pepper in medium saucepan. Bring to a boil over low heat, stirring occasionally to dissolve sugar. Pour over vegetables; mix gently. Chill, covered, for 24 hours.

The Brookwood Station ~ 1918

Meats

CHICAGO ITALIAN BEEF

Yield:
12 servings

Approx Per
Serving:
Cal 227
Prot 28 g
Carbo 1 g
T Fat 12 g
48% Calories
from Fat
Chol 95 mg
Fiber <1 g
Sod 455 mg

1 (3-pound to 4-pound)
  beef chuck roast
1 green bell pepper,
  chopped
1 small onion, chopped
2 teaspoons garlic
  powder
1 teaspoon rosemary

1 teaspoon caraway seeds
1 teaspoon celery salt
1¹/₂ teaspoons salt
2 teaspoons oregano
1 teaspoon marjoram
¹/₄ teaspoon red pepper
  flakes

Place chuck roast in 9x13-inch baking pan. Sprinkle with mixture of green pepper, onion, garlic powder, rosemary, caraway seeds, celery salt, salt, oregano, marjoram and red pepper flakes. Cover with water. Bake, covered, for 5 hours. Check water level, adding additional water if needed. Bake, covered, for 1 hour. Serve on Italian bread or rolls.

POT ROAST WITH CRANBERRY SAUCE

Yield:
6 servings

Approx Per
Serving:
Cal 573
Prot 72 g
Carbo 26 g
T Fat 19 g
30% Calories
from Fat
Chol 214 mg
Fiber 3 g
Sod 356 mg

1 (3¹/₂-pound to
  5-pound) beef brisket
Salt to taste
4 large onions, sliced
1 (8-ounce) can tomato
  sauce

1 (8-ounce) can whole
  cranberry sauce
Garlic powder to taste
Dillweed to taste
Oregano to taste

Brown brisket on all sides in salted saucepan. Remove brisket to platter. Sauté onions in pan drippings until tender. Return brisket to saucepan. Add tomato sauce, cranberry sauce, garlic powder, dillweed and oregano; mix well. Cook for 2¹/₂ hours. Slice brisket when cool. Reheat before serving. Store brisket and sauce separately in refrigerator; skim fat before reheating.

(Previous illustration) Brookwood Station is Atlanta's only remaining railway passenger station, presently listed as the Amtrak Passenger Station. A small garden on the south side features a statue of Samuel Spencer, the first president of the Southern Railway System.

AUTHENTIC GERMAN SAUERBRATEN

Yield:
8 servings

Approx Per
Serving:
Cal 204
Prot 19 g
Carbo 8 g
T Fat 7 g
31% Calories
from Fat
Chol 61 mg
Fiber 1 g
Sod 57 mg

1 carrot, finely chopped
1 stalk celery, finely chopped
1/2 leek, finely chopped
1 onion, finely chopped
2 whole cloves
1 bay leaf
6 peppercorns
6 juniper berries
1 1/2 cups red wine

1/4 cup wine vinegar
1 (1 3/4-pound) beef shoulder or rump roast
Salt and freshly ground pepper to taste
1 tablespoon butter
3 tablespoons raisins, rinsed
1 tablespoon lard
1 tablespoon flour

Bring carrot, celery, leek, onion, cloves, bay leaf, peppercorns, juniper berries, red wine and wine vinegar to a boil in a stainless steel saucepan, stirring occasionally. Immerse roast in mixture in bowl. Marinate, covered, in refrigerator for 3 to 5 days, turning occasionally. Drain, reserving marinade. Pat roast dry with paper towel; sprinkle with salt and pepper. Brown roast on all sides in butter in heavy saucepan. Add reserved marinade. Cook, covered, over low heat for 1 1/2 hours. Drain, reserving marinade; strain marinade. Return roast and strained marinade to saucepan. Stir in raisins. Melt lard in saucepan. Add flour, stirring until smooth. Cook until brown, stirring constantly. Stir 1 cup of marinade into lard mixture. Add mixture to saucepan. Cook over low heat for 15 minutes. Remove roast; thinly slice. Place on serving platter; drizzle roast with sauce. Serve remaining sauce with roast.

Jack Daniel's Marinade

Baste steaks, chicken and pork chops with mixture of 1/2 cup pineapple juice, 3 tablespoons soy sauce, 1 1/2 teaspoons ginger, 1/2 teaspoon garlic powder and 1/4 cup Jack Daniel's whiskey and grill over hot coals until cooked through.

STOCKYARD TURKEY

Yield:
variable

Nutritional information for this recipe is not available.

1 slab beef ribs   **Corn bread stuffing**
Salt and pepper to taste

Season ribs with salt and pepper. Parboil ribs with enough water to cover in stockpot; drain. Slice slab into halves. Place 1 slab in baking dish. Spread with corn bread dressing or your favorite dressing. Top with remaining slab. Bake at 350 degrees for 1¹/₂ hours. Serve with cranberry sauce or spiced apples. May substitute pork ribs for beef ribs.

TERIYAKI STEAKS

Yield:
9 servings

Approx Per Serving:
Cal 263
Prot 29 g
Carbo 6 g
T Fat 14 g
47% Calories from Fat
Chol 80 mg
Fiber <1 g
Sod 2231 mg

2 to 3 pounds beef   2 teaspoons MSG
   sirloin steaks   2 teaspoons ginger
²/₃ cup soy sauce   2 teaspoons dry mustard
¹/₄ cup vegetable oil   2 tablespoons molasses
6 cloves of garlic, minced

Place steaks in shallow dish. Pour mixture of soy sauce, oil, garlic, MSG, ginger, dry mustard and molasses over steaks, tossing to coat. Marinate, covered, in refrigerator for 24 hours or longer, tossing occasionally. Drain, reserving marinade. Grill over hot coals until done to taste, basting with reserved marinade occasionally. May substitute beef chuck or beef round steaks for sirloin steaks.

Nutritional information includes marinade.

MARINATED FLANK STEAK

Yield:
4 servings

Approx Per Serving:
Cal 167
Prot 18 g
Carbo 3 g
T Fat 9 g
47% Calories from Fat
Chol 45 mg
Fiber <1 g
Sod 214 mg

1/3 cup light Italian salad dressing
1/4 cup fresh lemon juice
2 tablespoons red wine vinegar

3 cloves of garlic, crushed
2 bay leaves, crushed
3/4 teaspoon pepper
1 (1-pound) beef flank steak, trimmed

Combine salad dressing, lemon juice, wine vinegar, garlic, bay leaves and pepper in bowl; mix well. Reserve 1/4 cup of marinade. Pour remaining marinade over steak in shallow dish, tossing to coat. Marinate, covered with plastic wrap, in refrigerator for 1 to 2 hours, turning several times. Drain, discarding marinade. Place steak on foil-lined rack in broiler pan. Broil 4 inches from heat source for 5 to 6 minutes per side for medium or until done to taste, basting frequently with reserved marinade. Transfer steak to carving board. Let stand for 5 minutes. Slice steak diagonally across grain, reserving juices. Arrange on serving platter. Garnish with watercress or parsley sprigs. Drizzle with reserved juices. May grill steak over hot coals for 5 to 6 minutes per side for medium-well steak.

Nutritional information includes marinade.

STEAK LOUIE

Yield:
4 servings

Approx Per Serving:
Cal 598
Prot 46 g
Carbo 4 g
T Fat 39 g
60% Calories from Fat
Chol 188 mg
Fiber <1 g
Sod 249 mg

4 filet mignon or ribeye steaks
1/4 cup butter
Salt and pepper to taste

4 cloves of garlic, minced
1 cup sour cream
1 cup white wine

Spread both sides of steaks with enough butter to coat; sprinkle with salt and pepper to taste. Sear both sides of steaks in hot skillet. Broil in oven or grill over hot coals until done to taste. Sauté garlic in remaining butter in skillet. Stir in sour cream and white wine. Simmer until of desired consistency, stirring frequently. Arrange steaks in sauce. Simmer, covered, for 15 minutes. Place steaks on dinner plates; drizzle with sauce. Use only table wine in this recipe as cooking wine contains a large amount of sodium.

SHISH KABOBS

Yield:
6 servings

Approx Per
Serving:
Cal 142
Prot 21 g
Carbo 2 g
T Fat 5 g
35% Calories
from Fat
Chol 60 mg
Fiber <1 g
Sod 751 mg

1 cup water
1/4 cup red wine vinegar
1 tablespoon tomato
  paste
1 teaspoon garlic salt
1/2 teaspoon salt
1 teaspoon pepper
1 bay leaf
1/2 cup chopped
  jalapeño peppers
1 1/2 pounds beef sirloin
  steak, cut into cubes

Combine water, wine vinegar, tomato paste, garlic salt, salt, pepper, bay leaf and jalapeño peppers in shallow dish; mix well. Add beef, tossing to coat. Marinate, covered, overnight. Drain, discarding marinade. Thread beef on skewers. Grill over hot coals for 20 to 30 minutes or until done to taste. May substitute beef round steak for sirloin steak.

Nutritional information includes marinade.

LIGHTNING CHILI

Yield:
16 servings

Approx Per
Serving:
Cal 164
Prot 22 g
Carbo 3 g
T Fat 7 g
37% Calories
from Fat
Chol 64 mg
Fiber 1 g
Sod 377 mg

4 pounds beef, cut into
  bite-sized pieces
Chopped onion to taste
2 cloves of garlic, minced
1 tablespoon oregano
2 tablespoons (or more)
  chili powder
8 hot jalapeño peppers,
  chopped
4 (4-ounce) cans
  chopped green chilies
1 tablespoon cumin
2 cups hot water
Salt to taste

Sauté beef, onion and garlic in heavy saucepan until light brown. Add oregano, chili powder, jalapeño peppers, chilies, cumin, hot water and salt; mix well. Bring to a boil; reduce heat. Simmer for 2 to 3 hours or until of desired consistency, stirring occasionally.

BEEF STRIPS OVER RICE

Yield:
4 servings

Approx Per Serving:
Cal 315
Prot 25 g
Carbo 40 g
T Fat 6 g
17% Calories from Fat
Chol 60 mg
Fiber 2 g
Sod 474 mg

2 tablespoons flour
1 (15-ounce) can stewed tomatoes
1 envelope onion soup mix
1/2 cup water
1/4 teaspoon pepper
1 pound beef sirloin steak, cut into thin strips
2 cups hot cooked rice

Shake flour in oven cooking bag. Place bag in 9x13-inch baking pan. Add mixture of undrained tomatoes, soup mix, water and pepper to bag. Add steak strips, tossing to coat. Arrange ingredients in single layer in bag; seal tightly. Cut six 1/2-inch slits in top of bag. Bake at 350 degrees for 40 to 45 minutes or until beef is done to taste. Serve over hot cooked rice.

GOOD-LUCK STEW

Yield:
12 servings

Approx Per Serving:
Cal 229
Prot 24 g
Carbo 18 g
T Fat 7 g
26% Calories from Fat
Chol 56 mg
Fiber 3 g
Sod 897 mg

3 pounds beef round steak, cut into bite-sized pieces
2 tablespoons vegetable oil
1 1/2 large onions, chopped
3 cloves of garlic, minced
5 (10-ounce) cans tomatoes with green chilies
2 (4-ounce) cans chopped green chilies
2 cups water
2 teaspoons salt-free beef bouillon granules
2 (16-ounce) cans yellow hominy, drained

Brown round steak in oil in stockpot; drain. Add onions, garlic, tomatoes and green chilies; mix well. Simmer for 5 minutes, stirring occasionally. Stir in water, bouillon and hominy. Simmer, covered, for 3 hours, stirring occasionally. May freeze for future use.

Beef Stroganoff

Yield:
6 servings

Approx Per
Serving:
Cal 413
Prot 29 g
Carbo 28 g
T Fat 21 g
45% Calories
from Fat
Chol 120 mg
Fiber 3 g
Sod 572 mg

1¹/2 pounds beef round steak, cut into thin strips
¹/4 cup flour
Pepper to taste
¹/4 cup butter
1 (4-ounce) can sliced mushrooms, drained
¹/2 cup chopped onion
1 small clove of garlic, minced
1 (10-ounce) can beef broth
1 cup sour cream
3 cups hot cooked wide noodles

Coat steak strips with mixture of flour and pepper. Brown in skillet in butter. Add mushrooms, onion and garlic; mix well. Cook until light brown, stirring constantly. Stir in broth. Simmer, covered, for 1 hour or until steak is tender, stirring occasionally. Stir in sour cream gradually. Cook over low heat for 5 minutes, stirring frequently. Serve over hot cooked noodles.

Company Beef Stroganoff

Yield:
6 servings

Approx Per
Serving:
Cal 365
Prot 30 g
Carbo 9 g
T Fat 23 g
58% Calories
from Fat
Chol 117 mg
Fiber 1 g
Sod 812 mg

2 cups sliced fresh mushrooms
1 cup finely chopped onion
4 tablespoons butter
2 pounds beef sirloin steak, cut into 2¹/2-inch strips
3 beef bouillon cubes
1 cup boiling water
2 tablespoons flour
¹/2 cup water
2 tablespoons tomato paste
1 teaspoon dry mustard
¹/2 teaspoon salt
1 cup sour cream

Sauté mushrooms and onion in 3 tablespoons of the butter in skillet until brown. Remove mushroom mixture to platter. Add remaining butter to pan drippings. Add steak. Cook for 15 minutes or until brown, stirring frequently. Add mixture of bouillon cubes and 1 cup boiling water; mix well. Simmer, covered, for 45 minutes or until beef is tender, stirring occasionally. Stir in mixture of flour and ¹/2 cup water. Bring to a boil, stirring constantly; reduce heat. Stir in tomato paste, dry mustard and salt. Add mushroom mixture and sour cream; mix well. Cook just until heated through, stirring constantly. Serve over cooked rice or noodles.

BEEF AND BEAN BURRITOS

Yield:
12 servings

Approx Per Serving:
Cal 336
Prot 20 g
Carbo 29 g
T Fat 15 g
42% Calories from Fat
Chol 53 mg
Fiber 4 g
Sod 575 mg

1¹/₂ pounds ground beef
1 (15-ounce) can refried beans
1 (4-ounce) can mild or hot diced green chilies
12 (8-inch) flour tortillas
¹/₂ head iceberg lettuce, finely chopped
8 ounces Cheddar cheese, shredded
1 or 2 tomatoes, finely chopped

Brown ground beef in skillet, stirring until crumbly; drain. Stir in refried beans and chilies. Cook just until heated through, stirring frequently. Spread beef mixture on tortillas; roll to enclose filling. Top with lettuce, cheese and tomatoes. Serve with salsa.

SPINACH STEW

Yield:
6 servings

Approx Per Serving:
Cal 418
Prot 18 g
Carbo 7 g
T Fat 36 g
76% Calories from Fat
Chol 49 mg
Fiber 3 g
Sod 1098 mg

³/₄ cup vegetable oil
1 small onion, chopped
1 small tomato, chopped
¹/₂ (6-ounce) can tomato paste
1 (12-ounce) can corned beef, chopped
1 teaspoon ground red pepper
1 teaspoon salt
1 pound fresh spinach, chopped

Heat oil in skillet over medium heat for 1 minute. Sauté onion in oil until tender. Stir in tomato and tomato paste. Cook for 5 minutes, stirring frequently. Add corned beef, red pepper, salt and spinach; mix well. Cook, covered, over medium-low heat for 30 to 35 minutes or until of desired consistency, stirring occasionally. Serve over hot cooked rice. May substitute one 10-ounce package frozen chopped spinach for fresh spinach.

SURPRISE CASSEROLE

Yield:
6 servings

**Approx Per
Serving:**
*Cal 398
Prot 33 g
Carbo 59 g
T Fat 26 g
39% Calories
from Fat
Chol 181 mg
Fiber 1 g
Sod 1130 mg*

1 pound ground beef
Salt and pepper to taste
3/4 cup cubed Cheddar
cheese
1 (12-ounce) package
egg noodles, cooked,
drained

1 (10-ounce) can cream
of mushroom soup
1 (10-ounce) can cream
of celery soup
2 tablespoons grated
Parmesan cheese
1 cup bread crumbs

Combine ground beef, salt and pepper in bowl; mix well. Shape into bite-sized meatballs around cheese cubes. Sauté meatballs in skillet until brown on all sides, drain. Stir in noodles, soups and cheese. Spoon into lightly greased baking dish. Sprinkle with bread crumbs. Bake at 375 degrees for 45 minutes.

COMPANY MEATBALLS

Yield:
36 servings

**Approx Per
Serving:**
*Cal 72
Prot 5 g
Carbo 2 g
T Fat 5 g
62% Calories
from Fat
Chol 26 mg
Fiber <1 g
Sod 142 mg*

1 1/2 pounds lean ground
beef
1 1/2 cups soft bread
crumbs
1/2 cup chopped onion,
sautéed
1 cup half and half
1 egg, beaten
1/4 cup finely chopped
parsley
1 1/2 teaspoons salt

1/4 teaspoon ginger
Pepper to taste
Nutmeg to taste
2 tablespoons butter
2 tablespoons flour
2 tablespoons melted
butter
3/4 cup beef broth
1/2 teaspoon instant
coffee granules

Combine ground beef, bread crumbs, onion, half and half, egg, parsley, salt, ginger, pepper and nutmeg in bowl; mix well. Shape into thirty-six 1 1/2-inch meatballs. Cook in 2 tablespoons butter in skillet over medium heat until brown on all sides; drain. Combine flour and 2 table-spoons melted butter in saucepan, stirring until smooth. Add broth and coffee granules; mix well. Cook over medium heat until thickened, stirring constantly. Serve with meatballs. May freeze meatballs for future use. Serve as an appetizer or over noodles as a main entrée.

GRANNY'S MEAT LOAF

Yield:
8 servings

Approx Per Serving:
Cal 247
Prot 21 g
Carbo 11 g
T Fat 13 g
48% Calories from Fat
Chol 90 mg
Fiber 1 g
Sod 329 mg

1 1/2 pounds ground beef
1 onion, chopped
1/2 cup bread crumbs
1 (8-ounce) can tomato sauce
1/4 cup chopped green bell pepper
Salt and pepper to taste
1 egg, beaten
1 cup water
2 tablespoons vinegar
2 tablespoons brown sugar
2 tablespoons prepared mustard

Combine ground beef, onion, bread crumbs, 1/2 of the tomato sauce, green pepper, salt, pepper and egg in bowl; mix well. Shape into loaf. Place in loaf pan. Process water, vinegar, brown sugar, mustard and remaining tomato sauce in blender until blended. Pour over meat loaf. Bake at 350 degrees for 1 1/4 hours, basting occasionally.

POLYNESIAN MEAT ROLLS

Yield:
8 servings

Approx Per Serving:
Cal 302
Prot 22 g
Carbo 22 g
T Fat 13 g
40% Calories from Fat
Chol 92 mg
Fiber <1 g
Sod 741 mg

1 1/2 pounds beef ground round
1 egg, beaten
1/2 cup rice
1/2 cup soft bread crumbs
1/2 cup milk
1/2 cup chopped onion
1 clove of garlic, crushed
1 teaspoon salt
1/4 teaspoon pepper
1 tablespoon soy sauce
2 cups beef broth
1 (6-ounce) can sweet and sour sauce

Combine ground round, egg, rice, bread crumbs, milk, onion, garlic, salt, pepper and soy sauce in bowl; mix well. Shape into individual rolls. Arrange in single layer in shallow baking dish. Pour broth over top. Bake, covered, at 350 degrees for 1 1/2 hours. Spoon sweet and sour sauce over beef rolls. Bake, uncovered, for 15 to 20 minutes or until bubbly.

POOR BOY'S ONE-DISH MEAL

Yield:
10 servings

Approx Per Serving:
Cal 350
Prot 24 g
Carbo 29 g
T Fat 17 g
41% Calories from Fat
Chol 69 mg
Fiber 6 g
Sod 702 mg

1 cup chopped onion
1/2 cup chopped green
  bell pepper
1/4 cup chopped celery
1/2 cup water
1 1/2 pounds ground beef
Salt and pepper to taste
2 (16-ounce) cans pork
  and beans

5 biscuits, baked, split
  into halves
1 cup shredded Cheddar
  cheese
1 (8-ounce) can tomato
  sauce

Combine onion, green pepper, celery and water in skillet; mix well. Simmer until vegetables are tender, stirring occasionally. Add ground beef, stirring until well mixed. Season with salt and pepper. Spread pork and beans in bottom of 10x10-inch baking dish. Layer ground beef mixture, biscuits and cheese in order listed over beans. Pour tomato sauce over top. Bake at 350 degrees for 45 minutes or until ground beef is cooked through.

STUFFED PASTA SHELLS

Yield:
6 servings

Approx Per Serving:
Cal 949
Prot 56 g
Carbo 90 g
T Fat 43 g
40% Calories from Fat
Chol 150 mg
Fiber 9 g
Sod 1842 mg

1 1/4 pounds ground beef
1 (32-ounce) can tomato
  paste
1 teaspoon garlic powder
1 tablespoon parsley
  flakes
1 teaspoon pepper
1 (4-ounce) can sliced
  black olives, drained

1 green bell pepper,
  chopped
1 medium onion,
  chopped
1 (16-ounce) package
  jumbo pasta shells,
  cooked, drained
16 ounces mild Cheddar
  cheese, shredded

Brown ground beef in skillet, stirring until crumbly; drain. Stir in 1/2 of the tomato paste, garlic powder, parsley flakes, pepper, black olives, green pepper and onion. Simmer for 6 to 8 minutes or until heated through. Stuff pasta shells with ground beef mixture. Place shells seam side down in 9x13-inch baking dish sprayed with nonstick cooking spray. Spoon remaining tomato paste over shells; sprinkle with cheese. Bake at 350 degrees for 15 to 20 minutes or until cheese melts. Serve with tossed vegetable salad.

ABSOLUTE BEST SPAGHETTI SAUCE

Yield:
16 servings

Approx Per Serving:
Cal 227
Prot 12 g
Carbo 22 g
T Fat 11 g
43% Calories from Fat
Chol 32 mg
Fiber 3 g
Sod 847 mg

1 pound ground beef
1 pound mild Italian sausage
8 ounces fresh mushrooms, sliced
1 onion, chopped
1 green bell pepper, chopped
1 stalk celery, chopped
1 (32-ounce) jar extra-thick spaghetti sauce
1 (15-ounce) can tomato sauce
2 (6-ounce) cans tomato paste
2 tomato paste cans water
1 (16-ounce) can whole tomatoes
2 cloves of garlic, minced
2 tablespoons oregano
Salt and pepper to taste
Garlic powder to taste
1/4 cup sugar

Brown ground beef and sausage in stockpot, stirring until crumbly; drain. Stir in remaining ingredients. Simmer for 3 to 4 hours or until of desired consistency, stirring occasionally. Serve over hot cooked spaghetti. May freeze for future use.

SPAGHETTI SAUCE

Yield:
10 servings

Approx Per Serving:
Cal 343
Prot 26 g
Carbo 24 g
T Fat 17 g
43% Calories from Fat
Chol 74 mg
Fiber 5 g
Sod 1423 mg

2 pounds ground beef
1 onion, chopped
1/4 green bell pepper, chopped
2 (20-ounce) cans tomatoes
2 (6-ounce) cans tomato paste
1 (46-ounce) can tomato juice
1 (3-ounce) package sliced pepperoni
1 (6-ounce) can mushrooms
1 bay leaf
1 teaspoon garlic salt
1/2 teaspoon red pepper flakes
1/4 cup sugar
1 teaspoon basil
2 teaspoons oregano
Steak sauce to taste
Cracker meal to taste

Brown ground beef with onion and green pepper in stockpot, stirring until ground beef is crumbly; drain. Stir in next 12 ingredients. Simmer for 5 hours or longer, stirring occasionally. Sprinkle with cracker meal 30 minutes before serving; stir. Skim off fat. Discard bay leaf.

RED-NECK STEW

Yield:
10 servings

Approx Per
Serving:
Cal 355
Prot 21 g
Carbo 46 g
T Fat 11 g
26% Calories
from Fat
Chol 51 mg
Fiber 6 g
Sod 703 mg

1¹/2 pounds ground beef
1 medium head
  cabbage, chopped
4 large onions, chopped
2 large green bell
  peppers, chopped
1 package chili-style
  Hamburger Helper
2 (16-ounce) cans
  tomatoes

3 medium potatoes,
  chopped
3 large carrots, chopped
1 (8-ounce) can
  cream-style corn
1 cup green beans
¹/2 teaspoon red pepper
Salt to taste

Combine ground beef, cabbage, onions, green peppers, Hamburger Helper, tomatoes, potatoes, carrots, corn, green beans, red pepper and salt in stockpot; mix well. Add just enough water to cover mixture; mix well. Bring to a boil; reduce heat. Simmer for 3 hours, stirring occasionally.

PARTY ROLLS

Yield:
24 servings

Approx Per
Serving:
Cal 161
Prot 7 g
Carbo 15 g
T Fat 8 g
46% Calories
from Fat
Chol 12 mg
Fiber 1 g
Sod 344 mg

2 (12-count) packages
  small French-style
  brown-and-serve rolls
8 ounces thinly sliced
  ham, cut into quarters
6 ounces Swiss cheese,
  thinly sliced, cut into
  quarters

¹/2 cup margarine
1 tablespoon onion flakes
1¹/2 teaspoons
  Worcestershire sauce
1¹/2 teaspoons prepared
  mustard

Slice rolls horizontally into halves; do not separate rolls. Place bottom half of rolls on baking sheet. Arrange ham and cheese slices over rolls; top with remaining roll halves. Melt margarine in saucepan. Stir in onion flakes, Worcestershire sauce and mustard; drizzle over rolls. Let stand for 20 minutes. Bake at 350 degrees for 35 minutes. Serve hot. May store, covered with waxed paper, in refrigerator until ready to bake.

SPICED PINEAPPLE PORK ROAST

Yield:
12 servings

Approx Per Serving:
Cal 272
Prot 29 g
Carbo 24 g
T Fat 7 g
23% Calories from Fat
Chol 73 mg
Fiber <1 g
Sod 104 mg

1 (4-pound) pork loin roast
1 (12-ounce) jar pineapple preserves
2 tablespoons honey
2 tablespoons red wine vinegar
1 teaspoon prepared mustard

$1/4$ teaspoon salt
$1/4$ teaspoon cinnamon
$1/4$ teaspoon ground cloves
1 (8-ounce) can pineapple slices, drained

Place pork roast on rack in shallow roasting pan. Insert meat thermometer into thickest part of roast. Roast at 350 degrees for $2^1/2$ to 3 hours or until meat thermometer registers 170 degrees. Combine preserves, honey, wine vinegar, mustard, salt, cinnamon and cloves in saucepan; mix well. Cook over low heat until preserves melt, stirring constantly. Arrange pineapple slices on pork roast and brush with pineapple glaze 20 minutes before end of cooking cycle. Serve remaining warm pineapple glaze with pork roast.

GREEN CHILE

Yield:
15 servings

Approx Per Serving:
Cal 215
Prot 27 g
Carbo 6 g
T Fat 8 g
36% Calories from Fat
Chol 74 mg
Fiber 1 g
Sod 443 mg

1 (5-pound) pork butt roast
1 large onion, cut into quarters
1 teaspoon salt
2 cloves of garlic, crushed
$1/4$ cup vegetable oil

1 (16-ounce) can whole tomatoes, mashed
1 (4-ounce) can jalapeño peppers, chopped
1 (4-ounce) can chopped green chilies
$1/2$ cup flour
1 teaspoon cumin

Combine pork roast, onion and salt with enough water to cover in stockpot. Cook until pork roast is cooked through. Drain, reserving liquid. Chop pork into bite-sized pieces. Sauté garlic in oil in stockpot until brown. Add tomatoes, jalapeño peppers and green chilies; mix well. Add flour, stirring until well mixed. Add reserved liquid as needed for desired consistency; mix well. Mix in cumin. Stir in chopped pork. Simmer for 1 hour, stirring occasionally.

SAUSAGE GUMBO

Yield:
4 servings

Approx Per Serving:
Cal 544
Prot 22 g
Carbo 82 g
T Fat 20 g
30% Calories from Fat
Chol 38 mg
Fiber 17 g
Sod 1840 mg

1 (16-ounce) package smoked sausage links
2 (15-ounce) cans Veg-All, drained
2 (16-ounce) cans whole kernel corn, drained
1 (16-ounce) package frozen okra

1 (16-ounce) can stewed tomatoes
1 medium onion, chopped
1/2 teaspoon gumbo filé
Salt and pepper to taste

Combine sausage, Veg-All, corn, okra, undrained tomatoes and onion in stockpot; mix well. Stir in gumbo filé after 5 minutes. Cook until onion is tender, stirring occasionally. Season with salt and pepper.

LASAGNA

Yield:
12 servings

Approx Per Serving:
Cal 604
Prot 36 g
Carbo 29 g
T Fat 39 g
57% Calories from Fat
Chol 157 mg
Fiber 3 g
Sod 1832 mg

1/2 cup chopped onion
3 to 4 cloves of garlic, crushed
2 tablespoons olive oil
2 pounds hot Italian sausage
1 tablespoon oregano
1 tablespoon basil
1 1/2 tablespoons salt
1/2 teaspoon pepper
1 (16-ounce) can tomatoes

2 (6-ounce) cans tomato paste
3 cups ricotta cheese
2 eggs, slightly beaten
1 (10-ounce) package lasagna noodles, cooked, drained
24 to 32 ounces mozzarella cheese, thinly sliced
1/2 cup grated Parmesan cheese

Sauté onion and garlic in olive oil in skillet until tender. Add sausage, stirring until sausage is crumbly; drain. Stir in seasonings, tomatoes and tomato paste. Simmer for 30 minutes or until of desired consistency, stirring occasionally. Combine ricotta cheese with eggs in bowl; mix well. Layer noodles, sausage mixture, ricotta cheese mixture, mozzarella cheese and Parmesan cheese 1/2 at a time in 9x13-inch baking dish. Bake at 375 degrees for 30 minutes. Let stand for 10 minutes before serving.

BREAKFAST BRUNCH

Yield:
10 servings

Approx Per Serving:
Cal 271
Prot 16 g
Carbo 12 g
T Fat 18 g
59% Calories from Fat
Chol 170 mg
Fiber <1 g
Sod 742 mg

1 pound bulk sausage
6 eggs
2 cups milk
1 teaspoon salt
1 teaspoon dry mustard
6 slices bread, torn into cubes

1 1/2 cups shredded Cheddar cheese
4 ounces mushrooms, sliced

Brown sausage in skillet, stirring until crumbly; drain. Let stand until cool. Beat eggs, milk, salt and dry mustard in mixer bowl until blended. Add bread cubes, stirring until moistened. Stir in cheese, mushrooms and sausage. Pour into greased 2-quart baking dish. Chill, covered, overnight. Bake at 350 degrees for 30 minutes.

BARBECUED VENISON

Yield:
40 servings

Approx Per Serving:
Cal 185
Prot 21 g
Carbo 5 g
T Fat 8 g
38% Calories from Fat
Chol 75 mg
Fiber <1 g
Sod 331 mg

1 (10-pound) venison roast, trimmed
2 cloves of garlic, minced
1 fifth dry red Claret wine
2 1/2 cups Worcestershire sauce
1 (10-ounce) can mushroom steak sauce

2 (4-ounce) jars whole mushrooms
1 cup corn oil
1 large green bell pepper, chopped
1 tablespoon pepper
Seasoned salt to taste

Place venison roast in large roasting pan. Pour mixture of garlic, wine, Worcestershire sauce, steak sauce, mushrooms, corn oil, green pepper, pepper and seasoned salt over roast. Bake at 350 degrees until venison is tender, basting every hour.

COUNTRY-FRIED VENISON WITH GRAVY

Yield:
6 servings

Approx Per Serving:
Cal 226
Prot 28 g
Carbo 10 g
T Fat 7 g
30% Calories from Fat
Chol 100 mg
Fiber <1 g
Sod 48 mg

2 pounds venison, cut into steaks
Salt and pepper to taste
1/2 cup flour

2 tablespoons shortening
2 tablespoons flour
Water

Tenderize steaks with meat mallet or saucer edge. Season with salt and pepper. Shake venison steaks with 1/2 cup flour in food storage bag until coated. Fry in shortening in skillet until brown on all sides. Remove steaks to serving platter. Drain skillet, reserving 2 tablespoons pan drippings. Add 2 tablespoons flour to pan drippings, stirring until smooth. Cook until brown, stirring constantly. Add water until of desired consistency; mix well. Simmer for 15 minutes or longer, stirring frequently. Serve gravy with venison steaks.

VENISON STEAKS

Yield:
4 servings

Approx Per Serving:
Cal 231
Prot 22 g
Carbo 8 g
T Fat 12 g
48% Calories from Fat
Chol 103 mg
Fiber <1 g
Sod 141 mg

1 pound (1/2-inch) venison steaks
1/4 cup evaporated milk
1/4 cup flour

3 tablespoons butter
Salt and pepper to taste
Garlic salt to taste

Tenderize steaks with meat mallet; cut into bite-sized pieces. Dip in evaporated milk; coat with flour. Brown 1 side of venison in butter in skillet; turn venison. Season with salt, pepper and garlic salt to taste. Cook until brown and tender.

Dogwood

Atlanta & West Point No. 290

Poultry and Seafood

SUNSHINE BARBECUED CHICKEN

Yield:
4 servings

Approx Per Serving:
Cal 413
Prot 54 g
Carbo 13 g
T Fat 15 g
33% Calories from Fat
Chol 161 mg
Fiber 1 g
Sod 665 mg

2 tablespoons flour
1 cup barbecue sauce
1/4 cup orange juice

8 pieces of chicken, skinned

Shake flour in 14x20-inch oven baking bag; place bag in 9x13-inch baking pan. Add barbecue sauce and orange juice to bag; squeeze to mix well. Rinse chicken and pat dry. Add to bag, turning to coat well. Arrange chicken in even layer in bag. Secure bag with nylon cord; cut six 1/2-inch slits in top of bag. Bake at 350 degrees for 45 to 50 minutes or until tender.

FIREHOUSE CHICKEN

Yield:
6 servings

Approx Per Serving:
Cal 636
Prot 46 g
Carbo 35 g
T Fat 35 g
49% Calories from Fat
Chol 135 mg
Fiber 4 g
Sod 1570 mg

1 (2 1/2-pound to 3-pound) chicken
Salt to taste
1 medium onion, chopped
1 (8-ounce) package tortilla chips, crushed
1 1/2 cups shredded Cheddar cheese

1 (10-ounce) can cream of mushroom soup
1 (10-ounce) can cream of chicken soup
1 (10-ounce) can tomatoes with green chilies

Rinse chicken well. Cook in salted water to cover in saucepan until tender. Remove chicken, reserving 3/4 cup broth. Chop chicken into bite-sized pieces, discarding skin and bones. Place in lightly greased shallow 2-quart baking dish. Layer onion, half the chips, cheese and remaining chips over chicken. Combine soups, tomatoes and reserved chicken broth in bowl; mix well. Spread over casserole. Bake at 350 degrees for 30 minutes.

GREEK ROAST CHICKEN

Yield:
6 servings

**Approx Per
Serving:**
*Cal 705
Prot 60 g
Carbo 38 g
T Fat 35 g
44% Calories
from Fat
Chol 173 mg
Fiber 4 g
Sod 816 mg*

1 (4-pound to 5-pound) chicken, cut up
Juice of 1¹/₂ lemons
3 tablespoons olive oil
¹/₂ tablespoon coarse-grain sea salt
2 pounds potatoes, cut lengthwise into quarters
6 cloves of garlic, unpeeled, slightly crushed
6 bay leaves
¹/₄ cup oregano
Pepper to taste
2 to 5 tablespoons olive oil
1 tablespoon unsalted butter
1³/₄ cups fat-free chicken broth
¹/₂ teaspoon Dijon mustard
1 teaspoon honey
¹/₂ cup coarsely chopped flat-leaf parsley

Rinse chicken, discarding skin and bones; pat dry. Rub with some of the lemon juice and 3 tablespoons olive oil; sprinkle with sea salt. Place in deep heavy baking dish. Arrange potatoes and garlic in single layer around chicken. Sprinkle with bay leaves, oregano, pepper and remaining olive oil; dot with butter. Add chicken broth. Roast at 375 degrees for 15 minutes. Reduce oven temperature to 350 degrees. Roast chicken for 40 minutes or until tender, basting frequently. Remove chicken and potatoes to serving platter. Strain 1¹/₂ cups pan drippings into small saucepan. Stir in mustard, honey and remaining lemon juice. Drizzle over chicken and potatoes; sprinkle with parsley.

Zesty Broiled Chicken

Sprinkle skinned chicken quarters or pieces with lemon or orange juice, chopped fresh rosemary, pepper and minced garlic. Broil for 25 to 35 minutes, turning once. Coat with Dijon mustard and broil for 2 to 4 minutes longer or until browned.

SMOTHERED FRIED CHICKEN

Yield:
6 servings

Approx Per
Serving:
Cal 351
Prot 26 g
Carbo 8 g
T Fat 24 g
61% Calories
from Fat
Chol 75 mg
Fiber <1 g
Sod 606 mg

1 (2¹/₄-pound) chicken, cut up
¹/₂ cup flour
1¹/₂ teaspoons salt
³/₄ teaspoon pepper
¹/₂ cup shortening
2 cups water

Rinse chicken and pat dry. Coat with mixture of flour, salt and pepper. Brown on both sides in shortening in large skillet; drain. Add water. Simmer, covered, for 30 to 40 minutes or until tender.

Nutritional information includes entire amount of shortening for frying.

BUTTERMILK PECAN CHICKEN FINGERS

Yield:
6 servings

Approx Per
Serving:
Cal 507
Prot 34 g
Carbo 23 g
T Fat 32 g
55% Calories
from Fat
Chol 137 mg
Fiber 3 g
Sod 490 mg

6 chicken breast filets
1 cup flour
1 cup pecans, toasted, ground
¹/₄ cup sesame seeds
1 tablespoon paprika
³/₄ teaspoon salt
¹/₈ teaspoon pepper
1 egg, slightly beaten
1 cup buttermilk
¹/₃ cup melted butter or margarine

Rinse chicken and pat dry. Cut each chicken breast into 4 strips. Combine flour, pecans, sesame seeds, paprika, salt and pepper in bowl. Beat egg and buttermilk in bowl. Dip chicken into egg mixture; coat with flour mixture. Arrange in melted butter in 10x15-inch baking pan, turning to coat well. Bake at 375 degrees for 30 minutes; drain. Garnish with lettuce and lemon slices.

COUNTRY-STYLE CHICKEN KIEV

Yield:
4 servings

Approx Per Serving:
Cal 488
Prot 30 g
Carbo 10 g
T Fat 35 g
65% Calories from Fat
Chol 158 mg
Fiber 1 g
Sod 935 mg

1/2 cup bread crumbs
2 tablespoons grated Parmesan cheese
1 teaspoon basil
1 teaspoon oregano
1/4 teaspoon salt
1/2 teaspoon garlic salt
4 chicken breasts
2/3 cup melted butter
1/4 cup white wine or apple juice
1/4 cup chopped green onions
1/4 cup chopped parsley

Combine bread crumbs, cheese, basil, oregano, salt and garlic salt in bowl; mix well. Rinse chicken and pat dry. Dip into butter; coat with crumb mixture. Arrange skin side up into shallow 1 1/2-quart baking dish. Bake at 375 degrees for 50 to 60 minutes or until tender. Add wine, green onions and parsley to remaining butter in bowl. Drizzle over chicken. Bake for 2 to 3 minutes longer. Though not boned and rolled like true Chicken Kiev, this chicken dish tastes surprisingly like the original.

CRESCENT ROLLS AND CHICKEN

Yield:
4 servings

Approx Per Serving:
Cal 500
Prot 28 g
Carbo 40 g
T Fat 25 g
46% Calories from Fat
Chol 82 mg
Fiber 1 g
Sod 1382 mg

2 chicken breast filets
Salt to taste
1/2 cup chopped onion
1/2 cup thawed frozen peas
1 (8-count) can crescent rolls
1 (10-ounce) can cream of mushroom soup
1 cup shredded Cheddar cheese
1 (5-ounce) can evaporated milk
Pepper to taste

Cook chicken in salted water to cover in saucepan until tender; drain. Chop chicken into very small pieces. Combine with onion and peas in bowl. Separate roll dough into triangles. Spoon chicken mixture onto triangles. Roll up to enclose filling; arrange in 8x12-inch baking pan sprayed with nonstick cooking spray. Combine soup, cheese and evaporated milk in bowl; mix well. Spoon over rolls; sprinkle with pepper. Bake at 350 degrees for 20 to 30 minutes or until bubbly and golden brown. May substitute turkey for chicken or add green bell pepper or mushrooms if desired.

GREEK-STYLE BAKED CHICKEN

Yield:
4 servings

Approx Per
Serving:
Cal 195
Prot 29 g
Carbo 2 g
T Fat 8 g
36% Calories
from Fat
Chol 86 mg
Fiber <1 g
Sod 236 mg

4 chicken breast filets
1 Roma or plum
   tomato, finely chopped
2 tablespoons chopped
   parsley
2 tablespoons chopped
   yellow or red bell
   pepper
1/4 cup crumbled feta
   cheese

1 tablespoon chopped
   fresh mint or 1/2
   teaspoon dried mint
1/4 teaspoon oregano
Freshly ground pepper
   to taste
1 teaspoon extra-virgin
   olive oil

Rinse chicken and pat dry; arrange in baking dish sprayed with olive-oil flavored cooking spray. Combine tomato, parsley, bell pepper, cheese, mint, oregano and pepper in bowl; mix well. Spoon over chicken; drizzle with olive oil. Bake at 375 degrees for 25 minutes or until chicken is tender. Serve over pasta or rice, with sauce spooned over top. Feta cheese does not melt like other cheese, so even when cooked, it holds its shape.

ITALIAN CHICKEN

Yield:
6 servings

Approx Per
Serving:
Cal 183
Prot 28 g
Carbo 9 g
T Fat 3 g
17% Calories
from Fat
Chol 72 mg
Fiber 3 g
Sod 310 mg

6 chicken breast filets
2 (16-ounce) cans
   Italian tomatoes
1 large onion, chopped

1 green bell pepper,
   chopped
1/2 teaspoon basil
1/4 teaspoon pepper

Rinse chicken and pat dry; arrange in 9x13-inch baking dish sprayed with nonstick cooking spray. Combine tomatoes, onion, green pepper, basil and pepper in bowl; mix well. Spread over chicken. Bake, covered, at 350 degrees for 1 hour. May serve over rice. This recipe is also good with fish.

LEMON BROCCOLI CHICKEN

Yield:
4 servings

Approx Per Serving:
Cal 253
Prot 28 g
Carbo 7 g
T Fat 12 g
43% Calories from Fat
Chol 74 mg
Fiber <1 g
Sod 608 mg

4 (4-ounce) chicken breast filets
1 tablespoon vegetable oil
1 (10-ounce) can cream of broccoli soup
1/4 cup milk
2 teaspoons lemon juice
1/8 teaspoon pepper
4 thin lemon slices

Rinse chicken and pat dry. Brown on both sides in heated oil in skillet; drain. Combine soup and milk in bowl; mix well. Stir in lemon juice and pepper. Spread over chicken; top with lemon slices. Simmer, covered, for 5 minutes or until chicken is tender, stirring occasionally.

PARMESAN CHICKEN

Yield:
10 servings

Approx Per Serving:
Cal 336
Prot 32 g
Carbo 15 g
T Fat 16 g
43% Calories from Fat
Chol 103 mg
Fiber 1 g
Sod 898 mg

2 cups bread crumbs
3/4 cup grated Parmesan cheese
1 cup chopped parsley
1/4 teaspoon garlic powder
2 teaspoons salt
10 chicken breast filets
1/2 cup melted butter

Combine bread crumbs, cheese, parsley, garlic powder and salt in bowl; mix well. Rinse chicken and pat dry. Dip into melted butter; coat with bread crumb mixture. Arrange in single layer in large baking pan lined with foil; drizzle with remaining butter. Bake at 350 degrees on middle oven rack for 1 hour.

CHICKEN AND RICE CASSEROLE

Yield:
8 servings

Approx Per
Serving:
Cal 477
Prot 32 g
Carbo 37 g
T Fat 22 g
41% Calories
from Fat
Chol 80 mg
Fiber 1 g
Sod 1216 mg

1/2 cup margarine
Seasoned salt to taste
1 (10-ounce) can cream
of mushroom soup
1 (10-ounce) can cream
of chicken soup

1 (10-ounce) can cream
of celery soup
1 (8-ounce) can
mushrooms, drained
1 1/2 cups uncooked rice
8 chicken breast filets

Melt margarine in 9x13-inch baking dish in 350-degree oven. Add salt, soups, mushrooms and rice. Rinse chicken and pat dry. Arrange over rice mixture. Bake, covered with foil, at 350 degrees for 45 minutes. Bake, uncovered, for 15 minutes longer.

CHICKEN DIVAN

Yield:
8 servings

Approx Per
Serving:
Cal 617
Prot 28 g
Carbo 27 g
T Fat 44 g
64% Calories
from Fat
Chol 116 mg
Fiber 3 g
Sod 1284 mg

2 (10-ounce) packages
frozen broccoli
4 chicken breasts,
cooked, chopped
2 (10-ounce) cans cream
of chicken soup
3/4 cup mayonnaise
1 teaspoon lemon juice
1/4 cup sherry

1/2 teaspoon curry
powder
2 cups shredded sharp
Cheddar cheese
1/2 loaf sandwich bread,
cubed
1/2 cup butter, sliced
1/4 cup Italian bread
crumbs

Cook broccoli using package directions just until tender; drain. Arrange in deep 8x12-inch baking dish. Sprinkle chicken over broccoli. Combine soup, mayonnaise, lemon juice, wine and curry powder in bowl; mix well. Spread over chicken; sprinkle with half the cheese. Combine bread cubes and butter in large saucepan. Cook over medium heat until butter melts, shaking saucepan constantly. Spread over casserole. Top with remaining cheese and Italian bread crumbs. Bake, covered, at 350 degrees for 25 to 30 minutes or until bubbly. Bake, uncovered, for 5 minutes longer or until brown.

CHICKEN AND DRESSING

Yield:
12 servings

Approx Per
Serving:
Cal 619
Prot 32 g
Carbo 53 g
T Fat 30 g
44% Calories
from Fat
Chol 221 mg
Fiber 3 g
Sod 1495 mg

1¹/2 cups self-rising flour
¹/4 cup vegetable oil
¹/2 cup milk
3 cups self-rising
  cornmeal
1 egg
¹/3 cup vegetable oil
2 cups milk
1 teaspoon sugar
1 teaspoon salt
8 chicken breasts
6 cups water

Salt to taste
¹/2 cup margarine
2 onions, chopped
5 slices loaf bread
8 eggs
2 (10-ounce) cans cream
  of chicken soup
1 cup milk
3 tablespoons sage
1 teaspoon celery seeds
1 tablespoon pepper

Combine flour, ¹/4 cup oil and ¹/2 cup milk in bowl; mix well. Drop by spoonfuls onto baking sheet. Bake at 450 degrees for 10 to 12 minutes or until biscuits are golden brown. Combine cornmeal, 1 egg, ¹/3 cup oil, 2 cups milk, sugar and 1 teaspoon salt in bowl; mix well. Spoon into greased baking pan. Bake at 450 degrees for 20 to 25 minutes. Rinse chicken well. Combine with water and salt to taste in large saucepan. Cook until tender. Remove chicken from broth and debone. Stir margarine and onions into broth. Simmer until onions are tender. Crumble biscuits, corn bread and loaf bread into large bowl. Add chicken broth, 8 eggs, soup, 1 cup milk, sage, celery seeds and pepper; mix well. Add chicken; mix gently. Spoon into greased baking pan. Bake at 350 degrees for 1 hour or until golden brown. May omit chicken and use dressing to stuff turkey. May substitute 3 stalks celery for celery seeds.

Gardenpatch Sandwich Spread

Mix 2 cups chopped cooked chicken or turkey with ¹/2 cup each minced carrots, celery, chopped pecans and 1 tablespoon minced green onion. Add a mixture of ¹/2 cup mayonnaise, 2 tablespoons sour cream, ¹/2 teaspoon curry powder and ¹/4 teaspoon salt. Mix well and chill for 2 hours to overnight.

CHICKEN CASSEROLE

Yield:
8 servings

Approx Per Serving:
Cal 366
Prot 20 g
Carbo 28 g
T Fat 20 g
48% Calories from Fat
Chol 40 mg
Fiber <1 g
Sod 1516 mg

4 chicken breasts
1 (10-ounce) can cream of mushroom soup
1 (10-ounce) can cream of chicken soup
1/2 cup margarine
1 (8-ounce) package herb-seasoned stuffing mix

Rinse chicken and pat dry. Cook in water to cover in saucepan until tender. Drain, reserving 3 cups broth. Chop chicken into bite-sized pieces, discarding skin and bones. Combine soups with 1 1/2 cups reserved chicken broth in saucepan; mix well. Bring to a boil; remove from heat. Stir in chicken. Spoon into 9x13-inch baking dish. Melt margarine in saucepan. Add remaining 1 1/2 cups chicken broth and stuffing mix; mix well. Sprinkle over casserole. Bake at 325 degrees for 30 minutes.

CHICKEN FETTUCINI

Yield:
6 servings

Approx Per Serving:
Cal 505
Prot 25 g
Carbo 45 g
T Fat 25 g
44% Calories from Fat
Chol 97 mg
Fiber 2 g
Sod 808 mg

12 ounces uncooked fettucini
2 cups chopped chicken
1 (4-ounce) can sliced mushrooms, drained
1/2 cup sliced celery
1/2 cup butter
1/2 cup light cream
1/2 cup grated Parmesan cheese
1 teaspoon salt
3/4 teaspoon pepper

Cook pasta using package directions; drain. Rinse chicken and pat dry. Sauté chicken, mushrooms and celery in butter in saucepan until chicken is cooked through and celery is tender. Stir in cream. Cook just until heated through; do not boil. Combine with hot pasta, cheese, salt and pepper in bowl; toss to mix well. Serve warm.

CHICKEN TETRAZZINI

Yield:
8 servings

Approx Per Serving:
Cal 519
Prot 34 g
Carbo 26 g
T Fat 30 g
52% Calories from Fat
Chol 146 mg
Fiber 1 g
Sod 557 mg

8 ounces uncooked vermicelli
8 ounces mushrooms, sliced
6 tablespoons butter
2 tablespoons flour
2 cups chicken broth
3 tablespoons dry sherry
1 cup whipping cream
Nutmeg, salt and pepper to taste
4 to 5 cups chopped cooked chicken
1/2 cup sliced black olives
1/2 cup grated Parmesan cheese

Cook pasta using package directions; drain. Sauté mushrooms in 3 tablespoons butter in skillet. Melt remaining 3 tablespoons butter in saucepan. Stir in flour. Cook until bubbly. Stir in chicken broth gradually. Cook until thickened, stirring constantly. Add wine, cream, nutmeg, salt and pepper. Cook for 10 minutes, stirring constantly. Combine half the sauce with pasta and mushrooms in saucepan; mix well. Spoon into buttered 3-quart baking dish. Add chicken and olives to remaining sauce; mix well. Spoon over pasta; sprinkle with cheese. Bake at 350 degrees for 30 minutes or until bubbly.

CHICKEN POTPIE

Yield:
6 servings

Approx Per Serving:
Cal 553
Prot 26 g
Carbo 44 g
T Fat 30 g
49% Calories from Fat
Chol 56 mg
Fiber 4 g
Sod 1356 mg

1 (16-ounce) can Veg-All, drained
2 (10-ounce) cans cream of chicken soup
4 chicken breasts, cooked, chopped
Salt and pepper to taste
2 deep-dish pie pastries

Combine mixed vegetables and soup in bowl; mix well. Stir in chicken, salt and pepper. Spoon into pastry-lined pie plate; top with remaining pastry. Bake at 350 degrees for 30 to 45 minutes or until golden brown.

NORTHERN TAMALES

Yield:
60 servings

Approx Per
Serving:
Cal 146
Prot 5 g
Carbo 8 g
T Fat 11 g
64% Calories
from Fat
Chol 12 mg
Fiber 1 g
Sod 109 mg

2¹/₂ cups shortening or
  lard
5 cups masa harina
  (corn flour)
4 cups warm water
6 cups chopped cooked
  chicken
4 cups chicken stock,
  pork stock or beef
  stock
2 tablespoons vegetable
  oil

¹/₂ cup chopped onion
2 cups chopped peeled
  tomatoes
2 (4-ounce) cans green
  chilies
4 cloves of garlic,
  crushed
¹/₂ teaspoon oregano
Salt and pepper to taste
1 or 2 packages
  cornhusks

Cut shortening into masa harina in large bowl until crumbly. Add warm water; mix well to form dough. Combine chicken, chicken stock, oil, onion, tomatoes, green chilies, garlic, oregano, salt and pepper in bowl; mix well. Spread 2 tablespoons dough on wider end of end of smooth side of cornhusk, spreading from left to right and only halfway down. Spread desired amount of filling along center of dough. Fold left side of cornhusk to center; fold right side to overlap left. Fold narrow pointed end of husk over filling to cover completely. Repeat with remaining ingredients. Stand tamales open end up on steaming rack in large heavy saucepan. Pour water carefully around sides almost to depth of rack; water should not touch tamales. Place damp towel across tamales. Bring to a boil over high heat. Reduce heat. Steam, covered, for 45 minutes, checking water after 20 minutes and adding more if needed. May crumple a large piece of heavy-duty foil to place in bottom of saucepan in place of steaming rack.

CHICKEN SOUTH OF THE BORDER

Yield:
8 servings

Approx Per Serving:
Cal 339
Prot 25 g
Carbo 22 g
T Fat 17 g
45% Calories from Fat
Chol 69 mg
Fiber 2 g
Sod 1267 mg

1 (10-ounce) can cream of chicken soup
1 (10-ounce) can cream of mushroom soup
1 soup can chicken broth or milk
1 (7-ounce) can chopped green chilies
1 small onion, chopped
1 (8-count) package corn tortillas, cut into bite-sized pieces
4 chicken breasts, cooked, chopped
2 cups shredded Cheddar cheese

Combine soups, chicken broth, green chilies and onion in bowl; mix well. Alternate layers of tortillas, chicken, cheese and soup mixture in greased large baking dish until all ingredients are used. Chill for 24 hours. Bake at 300 degrees for 1 to 1¹/2 hours or until bubbly and golden brown.

THE JUICIEST HOLIDAY TURKEY

Yield:
12 servings

Approx Per Serving:
Cal 521
Prot 90 g
Carbo 0 g
T Fat 15 g
28% Calories from Fat
Chol 232 mg
Fiber 0 g
Sod 214 mg

1 (8-pound to 15-pound) turkey
Salt and pepper to taste

Rinse turkey inside and out and pat dry. Sprinkle inside and out with salt and pepper. Place in oven-baking bag using package directions. Let stand in refrigerator for 2 days. Bake using bag instructions. May use cooking juices in dressing.

EASY STUFFED TURKEY CUTLETS

Yield:
4 servings

Approx Per Serving:
Cal 319
Prot 43 g
Carbo 9 g
T Fat 12 g
34% Calories from Fat
Chol 108 mg
Fiber 3 g
Sod 370 mg

1 pound fresh spinach, chopped
1¹/2 cups part-skim milk ricotta cheese
¹/3 cup chopped yellow onion
3 tablespoons grated Parmesan cheese
1 teaspoon olive oil
1 egg white, slightly beaten
8 (2-ounce) thin turkey cutlets
2 tablespoons reduced-sodium chicken broth

Mix first 5 ingredients in bowl. Reserve ¹/2 cup of the mixture. Add egg white to remaining spinach mixture. Rinse cutlets and pat dry. Spoon 2 tablespoons stuffing along long side of each cutlet. Roll cutlets to enclose stuffing, pressing edges to seal. Place seam side down in shallow baking dish sprayed with nonstick cooking spray. Bake at 350 degrees for 30 minutes or until cooked through. Process reserved spinach mixture and chicken broth in blender for 30 seconds or until smooth. Heat in saucepan over low heat for 2 minutes. Spoon 2 table-spoons heated sauce onto each serving plate. Slice cutlet rolls diagonally and arrange 2 in sauce on each plate.

TACO CASSEROLE

Yield:
6 servings

Approx Per Serving:
Cal 604
Prot 33 g
Carbo 49 g
T Fat 31 g
46% Calories from Fat
Chol 95 mg
Fiber 2 g
Sod 1773 mg

8 ounces Velveeta cheese, cubed
1 (10-ounce) can cream of mushroom soup
1 soup can skim milk
1 pound ground turkey
1 envelope taco seasoning mix
1 cup water
2 cups macaroni, cooked, drained
1 cup crushed chili-cheese flavor or barbecue-flavor corn chips

Combine cheese, soup and milk in saucepan or micro-wave-safe bowl. Heat or microwave just until cheese melts, stirring to mix well. Brown ground turkey in skillet, stirring until crumbly. Add taco seasoning mix and water; mix well. Cook until ³/4 of the water has evaporated. Add to cheese sauce with macaroni; mix gently. Spoon into 9x13-inch baking dish; top with crushed corn chips. Bake at 325 degrees for 20 minutes.

DEVILED CRAB

Yield:
8 servings

Approx Per
Serving:
Cal 361
Prot 30 g
Carbo 18 g
T Fat 19 g
47% Calories
from Fat
Chol 284 mg
Fiber 1 g
Sod 1308 mg

1/2 large onion, chopped
2 stalks celery, chopped
1 medium green bell
  pepper, chopped
2 tablespoons butter
2 pounds crab meat
1/4 cup mayonnaise

Tabasco sauce to taste
1 teaspoon dry mustard
2 teaspoons salt
1/2 cup catsup
6 eggs, beaten
2 cups butter cracker
  crumbs

Sauté onion, celery and green pepper in butter in skillet until tender. Stir in crab meat. Cook for 10 minutes, stirring occasionally. Stir in mayonnaise, Tabasco sauce, dry mustard, salt, catsup and eggs. Spoon into baking shells or into 9x13-inch baking dish; sprinkle with cracker crumbs. Bake at 350 degrees for 30 minutes.

QUICK HALIBUT

Yield:
6 servings

Approx Per
Serving:
Cal 405
Prot 37 g
Carbo 16 g
T Fat 21 g
47% Calories
from Fat
Chol 89 mg
Fiber 1 g
Sod 694 mg

2 tablespoons onion
  soup mix
1 cup sour cream
1 cup plain dry bread
  crumbs
2 tablespoons grated
  Parmesan cheese

1 tablespoon parsley
  flakes
1/4 teaspoon paprika
2 pounds (1/2-inch to
  3/4-inch) halibut filets
1/4 cup melted butter

Combine soup mix and sour cream in bowl; mix well. Combine bread crumbs, cheese, parsley flakes and paprika in bowl; mix well. Dip filets in soup mixture; dredge in bread crumb mixture. Arrange in baking pan; drizzle with butter. Bake at 500 degrees for 10 to 12 minutes or until fish flakes easily.

SALMON PATTIES

Yield:
6 servings

Approx Per
Serving:
Cal 165
Prot 18 g
Carbo 7 g
T Fat 7 g
37% Calories
from Fat
Chol 69 mg
Fiber 1 g
Sod 466 mg

1 (16-ounce) can
  salmon, drained, flaked
1 egg, beaten
1/3 cup buttermilk
1/3 cup finely chopped
  onion
1/3 cup cornmeal
1/4 teaspoon baking soda
Vegetable oil for frying

Combine salmon, egg, buttermilk, onion, cornmeal and baking soda in bowl; mix well. Shape into 6 patties. Fry in 1 1/2 to 2 inches oil in heavy skillet for 10 minutes or until brown on both sides, turning once; drain.

Nutritional information does not include oil for frying.

GRILLED SCALLOPS

Yield:
6 servings

Approx Per
Serving:
Cal 113
Prot 17 g
Carbo 3 g
T Fat 4 g
29% Calories
from Fat
Chol 35 mg
Fiber <1 g
Sod 489 mg

2 cloves of garlic, minced
1/4 cup lemon juice
2 tablespoons minced
  fresh parsley
3/4 teaspoon oregano
1 pound sea scallops
6 ounces smoked lean
  ham, sliced, cut into
  1/2-inch strips

Coat nonstick skillet with nonstick cooking spray. Heat over medium heat. Sauté garlic in skillet until brown. Remove from heat. Stir in lemon juice, parsley and oregano. Wrap each scallop with ham strip. Thread 6 scallops onto each skewer. Coat grill rack with nonstick cooking spray. Grill scallops over medium-hot coals for 9 minutes, basting frequently with lemon juice mixture.

SURIMI AND RED PEPPER PASTA

Yield:
6 servings

Approx Per Serving:
Cal 531
Prot 10 g
Carbo 18 g
T Fat 21 g
35% Calories from Fat
Chol 17 mg
Fiber <1 g
Sod 782 mg

1 pound fettucini
2 large red bell peppers
3 cloves of garlic, minced
6 tablespoons olive oil
1 cup lemon juice
6 teaspoons Dijon mustard
1 teaspoon dried basil or dillweed
1 pound surimi (faux crab)
1 to 2 tablespoons olive oil

Cook fettucini using package directions; rinse and drain. Set aside; keep warm. Cut red peppers into julienne strips. Sauté garlic in 6 tablespoons hot olive oil in large skillet over medium heat for 30 seconds. Add red pepper strips. Sauté for 1 to 2 minutes. Stir in lemon juice, mustard and basil. Simmer, covered, for 2 to 3 minutes. Add surimi. Cook for 1 to 2 minutes or until heated through, stirring constantly. Toss fettucini with 1 to 2 tablespoons olive oil; place on serving platter. Ladle sauce over top. Serve with grated Parmesan cheese if desired.

SHRIMP CREOLE

Yield:
6 servings

Approx Per Serving:
Cal 309
Prot 17 g
Carbo 40 g
T Fat 9 g
26% Calories from Fat
Chol 139 mg
Fiber 3 g
Sod 1018 mg

1 1/2 cups chopped onions
1 cup finely chopped celery
2 medium green bell peppers, finely chopped
2 cloves of garlic, minced
1/4 cup butter
1 (15-ounce) can tomato sauce
1 cup water
2 teaspoons snipped fresh parsley
1 teaspoon salt
1/8 teaspoon cayenne pepper
2 bay leaves, crushed
1 pound fresh or frozen peeled shrimp
3 cups hot cooked rice

Sauté onions, celery, green peppers and garlic in butter in saucepan until onions are tender. Remove from heat. Stir in tomato sauce, water, parsley, salt, cayenne pepper and bay leaves. Simmer for 10 minutes, stirring occasionally. Stir in additional water if needed for desired consistency. Stir in shrimp. Bring to a boil; reduce heat. Cook, covered, over medium heat for 10 to 20 minutes or until shrimp are pink. Serve over hot cooked rice.

SHRIMP AND CRAB MEAT CASSEROLE

Yield:
4 servings

Approx Per Serving:
Cal 742
Prot 40 g
Carbo 12 g
T Fat 60 g
72% Calories from Fat
Chol 289 mg
Fiber 1 g
Sod 1561 mg

1 onion, finely chopped
2 stalks celery, finely chopped
1 green bell pepper, finely chopped
2 tablespoons margarine
12 ounces cooked peeled shrimp
12 ounces crab meat, drained, flaked

1 cup mayonnaise
Worcestershire sauce to taste
1 (10-ounce) can cream of mushroom soup
Tabasco sauce to taste
Teriyaki sauce to taste
1/4 cup grated Parmesan cheese

Sauté onion, celery and green pepper in margarine in skillet. Stir in shrimp, crab meat, mayonnaise, Worcestershire sauce, soup, Tabasco sauce and teriyaki sauce. Spoon into baking dish. Sprinkle with Parmesan cheese. Bake at 350 degrees for 45 minutes.

SOUTHERN SHRIMP JAMBALAYA

Yield:
4 servings

Approx Per Serving:
Cal 193
Prot 20 g
Carbo 12 g
T Fat 8 g
35% Calories from Fat
Chol 166 mg
Fiber 2 g
Sod 555 mg

2 slices bacon, chopped
1 tablespoon flour
1 onion, chopped
1/2 green bell pepper, chopped
1 (16-ounce) can stewed tomatoes
1/2 teaspoon Worcestershire sauce

1/8 teaspoon cayenne pepper
1/4 teaspoon thyme
1 pound medium shrimp, peeled, deveined
Salt and black pepper to taste

Cook bacon in skillet for 3 minutes or until partially cooked, stirring constantly. Remove bacon to platter. Add flour to bacon drippings, stirring until smooth. Cook for 2 to 3 minutes or until brown, stirring constantly. Stir in onion and green pepper. Cook for 5 minutes or until onion is tender, stirring constantly. Add bacon, undrained tomatoes, Worcestershire sauce, cayenne pepper, thyme and shrimp; mix well. Bring to a boil; reduce heat. Simmer for 5 minutes or until shrimp are pink, stirring occasionally. Season with salt and black pepper. Serve over hot cooked rice. May substitute crab meat, oysters or bite-sized pieces of firm fish for shrimp.

LOW-COUNTRY BOIL

Yield:
15 servings

**Approx Per
Serving:**
Cal 620
Prot 45 g
Carbo 51 g
T Fat 27 g
39% Calories
from Fat
Chol 313 mg
Fiber 7 g
Sod 1060 mg

3 lemons, cut into quarters
2 bags shrimp and crab boil seasoning
3 pounds new red potatoes
6 pounds Polish sausage, sliced
20 ears of corn, broken into halves
6 pounds shrimp, heads removed

Combine lemons, shrimp and crab boil seasoning and unpeeled new potatoes with enough water to cover in stockpot. Cook until potatoes are partially cooked. Add sausage and corn. Bring to a boil. Cook for 10 minutes. Add shrimp. Cook until shrimp turn pink. Drain, discarding lemons and shrimp and crab boil bags. Spread mixture on newspaper-covered serving table for hungry guests to enjoy. Serve with saltine crackers, prepared mustard, butter and cocktail sauce. This recipe originated in the Low Country of South Carolina.

MARYLAND STEAMED SHRIMP

Yield:
6 servings

**Approx Per
Serving:**
Cal 183
Prot 34 g
Carbo 2 g
T Fat 2 g
9% Calories
from Fat
Chol 316 mg
Fiber <1 g
Sod 366 mg

1 (12-ounce) can beer
1 beer can water
3 pounds fresh or frozen unpeeled shrimp
Old Bay Seasoning to taste

Pour beer and water into stockpot. Layer shrimp and Old Bay Seasoning alternately in steamer rack until all ingredients are used. Place rack in stockpot. Bring to a boil. Boil, covered, for 8 to 10 minutes or until shrimp are pink.

SHRIMP- AND RICE-STUFFED PEPPERS

Yield:
8 servings

Approx Per
Serving:
Cal 434
Prot 27 g
Carbo 29 g
T Fat 24 g
49% Calories
from Fat
Chol 237 mg
Fiber 3 g
Sod 735 mg

8 green bell peppers
1 cup rice
2 pounds small cooked
  peeled shrimp
1 small onion, chopped

Tabasco sauce to taste
Salt and pepper to taste
1 cup mayonnaise
1 (15-ounce) can tomato
  sauce

Slice tops off green peppers; discard seeds. Place cut side down in boiling water in saucepan. Let stand until light in color; drain. Cook rice using package directions. Combine rice, shrimp, onion, Tabasco sauce, salt and pepper in bowl; mix well. Stir in mayonnaise. Stuff green peppers with rice mixture. Place in baking pan; drizzle with 3/4 of the tomato sauce. Bake at 350 degrees until heated through. Cut each green pepper into halves. Place on serving platter; drizzle with remaining tomato sauce.

SHRIMP AND PASTA STIR-FRY

Yield:
2 servings

Approx Per
Serving:
Cal 376
Prot 28 g
Carbo 50 g
T Fat 7 g
16% Calories
from Fat
Chol 177 mg
Fiber 4 g
Sod 726 mg

1/4 cup fat-free
  mayonnaise
1/4 cup low-sodium
  chicken broth
1 tablespoon lemon juice
2 teaspoons vegetable oil
1 tablespoon grated
  peeled gingerroot
1 clove of garlic, minced

8 ounces medium peeled
  shrimp
1 cup (1-inch)
  diagonally sliced fresh
  asparagus
2 cups hot cooked
  penne or zita
1/4 teaspoon lemon
  pepper

Combine mayonnaise, broth and lemon juice in bowl; mix well with wire whisk. Spray wok with nonstick cooking spray. Add oil. Heat over medium-high heat until hot. Stir-fry gingerroot and garlic in oil for 1 minute. Add shrimp and asparagus. Stir-fry for 3 minutes or until shrimp are pink. Stir in mayonnaise mixture and pasta. Cook just until heated through. Sprinkle with lemon pepper.

Tullie Smith House - 1840

❧

Vegetables and Side Dishes

BEAN CASSEROLE

Yield:
12 servings

Approx Per
Serving:
Cal 214
Prot 11 g
Carbo 31 g
T Fat 6 g
25% Calories
from Fat
Chol 22 mg
Fiber 6 g
Sod 757 mg

8 ounces ground beef
8 ounces bacon
1 cup minced onion
1/2 cup catsup
1 teaspoon salt
3/4 cup packed brown
  sugar
1 teaspoon dry mustard

2 tablespoons vinegar
1 (16-ounce) can kidney
  beans, drained
1 (16-ounce) can pork
  and beans, drained
1 (16-ounce) can
  French-style green
  beans, drained

Brown ground beef in skillet, stirring until crumbly; drain. Fry bacon in skillet until crisp; drain. Crumble bacon. Combine ground beef, bacon, onion, catsup, salt, brown sugar, dry mustard, vinegar and beans in bowl; mix well. Spoon into baking pan. Bake at 350 degrees for 1 hour.

GRANDMA'S BAKED BEANS

Yield:
12 servings

Approx Per
Serving:
Cal 457
Prot 28 g
Carbo 55 g
T Fat 15 g
29% Calories
from Fat
Chol 78 mg
Fiber 7 g
Sod 803 mg

2 1/2 pounds ground beef
1 medium onion,
  chopped
3 (16-ounce) cans pork
  and beans

1 1/2 cups catsup
1 1/2 cups packed brown
  sugar
1 tablespoon dry
  mustard

Brown ground beef with onion in skillet, stirring until ground beef is crumbly; drain. Stir in pork and beans, catsup, brown sugar and dry mustard. Spoon into 9x13-inch baking pan. Bake at 350 degrees for 1 hour.

(Previous illustration) The Tullie Smith House is one of the oldest houses in the Atlanta area. Built about 1835 by the Robert Smith family on land ceded to the state by the Creek Indians in 1821, it represents the typical plantation of a settler in the Piedmont region of Georgia. Located on the grounds of the Atlanta Historical Society, it is open to visitors Tuesday through Sunday.

MAMA'S BAKED BEANS

Yield:
8 servings

*Approx Per
Serving:*
Cal 216
Prot 7 g
Carbo 30 g
T Fat 9 g
*35% Calories
from Fat*
Chol 12 mg
Fiber 3 g
Sod 601 mg

1 (16-ounce) can
    ranch-style beans
1 (16-ounce) can pork
    and beans
1/4 cup packed brown
    sugar

1/4 cup catsup
1/2 envelope onion soup
    mix
1 tablespoon
    Worcestershire sauce
3 or 4 slices bacon

Combine beans, brown sugar, catsup, soup mix and Worcestershire sauce in bowl; mix well. Spoon into 1 1/2- to 2-quart baking dish. Top with bacon slices. Bake at 350 degrees for 1 hour or at 425 degrees for 35 to 40 minutes. May substitute Mexican chili beans for ranch-style beans.

BROCCOLI CASSEROLE

Yield:
8 servings

*Approx Per
Serving:*
Cal 460
Prot 21 g
Carbo 29 g
T Fat 30 g
*57% Calories
from Fat*
Chol 85 mg
Fiber 4 g
Sod 1256 mg

1 small onion, chopped
1/4 cup butter
3 (10-ounce) packages
    frozen chopped
    broccoli, cooked,
    drained
1 teaspoon salt
1 teaspoon pepper

8 ounces vermicelli,
    cooked, drained
16 ounces Velveeta
    cheese, sliced
1/2 cup half and half
1/4 cup grated Parmesan
    cheese
2 tablespoons butter

Sauté onion in 1/4 cup butter in skillet. Add mixture of broccoli, salt and pepper; mix well. Cook over low heat for 5 minutes, stirring occasionally. Layer vermicelli and 1/2 of the Velveeta cheese in 8x10-inch baking dish. Pour half and half over layers. Spread with broccoli mixture. Top with remaining Velveeta cheese; sprinkle with Parmesan cheese. Dot with 2 tablespoons butter. Bake, covered, at 350 degrees for 30 minutes.

BROCCOLI WITH CHEESE AND RICE

Yield:
6 servings

Approx Per
Serving:
Cal 349
Prot 10 g
Carbo 38 g
T Fat 18 g
46% Calories
from Fat
Chol 39 mg
Fiber 3 g
Sod 790 mg

1 onion, chopped
3 stalks celery, chopped
1/4 cup butter
4 ounces Velveeta
  cheese, shredded
Salt and pepper to taste
1/4 teaspoon oregano
1 teaspoon garlic powder
1/2 teaspoon basil

1 jalapeño pepper,
  chopped
2 to 3 cups cooked rice
1 (10-ounce) package
  frozen chopped
  broccoli, thawed,
  drained
1 (10-ounce) can cream
  of mushroom soup

Sauté onion and celery in butter in skillet until tender. Stir in cheese, salt, pepper, oregano, garlic powder, basil and jalapeño pepper. Add rice, broccoli and soup; mix well. Spoon into buttered baking dish. Bake at 350 degrees for 30 minutes.

CARROTS WITH HORSERADISH

Yield:
6 servings

Approx Per
Serving:
Cal 238
Prot 2 g
Carbo 17 g
T Fat 19 g
69% Calories
from Fat
Chol 21 mg
Fiber 4 g
Sod 318 mg

8 to 10 carrots, cut into
  3- to 4-inch slices
Salt to taste
1/2 cup mayonnaise
2 tablespoons grated
  onion
1/4 teaspoon salt

1/4 teaspoon pepper
3 tablespoons prepared
  horseradish
1/4 cup fine bread crumbs
1 to 2 tablespoons
  melted butter

Combine carrots and salt with enough water to cover in saucepan. Cook until tender-crisp. Drain, reserving 1/4 cup liquid. Cool carrots slightly. Cut into lengthwise strips. Arrange in 1 1/2-quart baking dish. Spoon mixture of reserved carrot liquid, mayonnaise, onion, salt, pepper and horseradish over carrots. Sprinkle with mixture of bread crumbs and butter. Bake, covered, at 375 degrees for 15 to 20 minutes or until bubbly, removing cover 5 minutes before end of cooking cycle.

FESTIVE CARROTS AND PINEAPPLE

Yield:
4 servings

Approx Per Serving:
Cal 143
Prot 1 g
Carbo 30 g
T Fat 3 g
19% Calories from Fat
Chol 8 mg
Fiber 2 g
Sod 306 mg

1 (8-ounce) can
  pineapple chunks
1/4 cup packed brown
  sugar
1 tablespoon butter

2 teaspoons cornstarch
1/2 teaspoon cinnamon
1 (16-ounce) can
  carrots, drained

Drain pineapple, reserving juice. Combine reserved juice, brown sugar, butter, cornstarch and cinnamon in saucepan. Cook until thickened, stirring constantly. Stir in pineapple and carrots. Cook just until heated through, stirring constantly. Garnish with grated lime rind.

POT-OF-GOLD CARROTS

Yield:
20 servings

Approx Per Serving:
Cal 112
Prot 1 g
Carbo 15 g
T Fat 6 g
45% Calories from Fat
Chol 0 mg
Fiber 2 g
Sod 122 mg

2 pounds carrots, sliced
Salt to taste
1 (10-ounce) can tomato
  soup
3/4 cup sugar
1/2 cup vinegar

1/2 cup vegetable oil
1 large green bell
  pepper, chopped
1 medium to large
  onion, chopped

Combine carrots and salt with enough water to cover in saucepan. Cook until tender-crisp; drain. Place in bowl. Combine soup, sugar, vinegar and oil in bowl; mix well. Stir in green pepper and onion. Pour mixture over carrots, tossing to coat. Marinate, covered, in refrigerator for 24 hours, tossing occasionally. May store in refrigerator for several weeks.

CREAMY CORN

Yield:
12 servings

Approx Per Serving:
Cal 527
Prot 7 g
Carbo 30 g
T Fat 45 g
73% Calories from Fat
Chol 42 mg
Fiber 2 g
Sod 955 mg

4 (15-ounce) cans corn, drained
16 ounces cream cheese, softened
2 cups margarine
1 or 2 jalapeño peppers, finely chopped

Combine corn, cream cheese, margarine and jalapeño peppers in slow cooker; mix well. Cook on High until hot, stirring occasionally. May microwave in microwave-safe bowl.

SCALLOPED CORN SOUFFLE

Yield:
8 servings

Approx Per Serving:
Cal 417
Prot 10 g
Carbo 39 g
T Fat 26 g
55% Calories from Fat
Chol 107 mg
Fiber 2 g
Sod 708 mg

1 medium onion, chopped
1/2 medium green bell pepper, chopped
1/2 cup margarine
1 (15-ounce) can cream-style corn
1 (15-ounce) can whole kernel corn
3 eggs, beaten
1 (7-ounce) package corn muffin mix
1 cup sour cream
1 cup shredded Cheddar cheese

Sauté onion and green pepper in margarine in skillet. Combine onion mixture, cream-style corn, undrained whole kernel corn, beaten eggs and corn muffin mix in bowl; mix well. Spoon into 2-quart baking dish. Spread with sour cream; sprinkle with cheese. Bake at 325 degrees for 1 hour.

EASY EGGPLANT PARMESAN

Yield:
6 servings

Approx Per Serving:
Cal 617
Prot 21 g
Carbo 50 g
T Fat 35 g
52% Calories from Fat
Chol 108 mg
Fiber 7 g
Sod 1737 mg

2 medium eggplant, peeled, cut into 1/3-inch slices
2 eggs, beaten
2 cups Italian-seasoned bread crumbs
1/2 cup extra-light olive oil
1 (28-ounce) jar spaghetti sauce with mushrooms
8 ounces mozzarella cheese, sliced
1/2 cup grated Parmesan cheese

Dip eggplant slices in eggs; coat with bread crumbs. Brown in olive oil in skillet; drain. Spread 1/2 of the spaghetti sauce in 9x13-inch baking dish. Layer eggplant and mozzarella cheese over sauce. Top with remaining spaghetti sauce; sprinkle with Parmesan cheese. Bake at 400 degrees for 20 minutes.

EL FEO

Yield:
8 servings

Approx Per Serving:
Cal 109
Prot 6 g
Carbo 19 g
T Fat 2 g
18% Calories from Fat
Chol 0 mg
Fiber 5 g
Sod 620 mg

1 clove of garlic, minced
1 tablespoon virgin olive oil
3 large yellow squash, sliced
2 medium tomatoes, sliced
6 to 8 large mushrooms, sliced
3 scallions, sliced
1 to 2 jalapeño peppers, seeded, chopped
1 tablespoon soy sauce
1 teaspoon salt
1 teaspoon pepper
1 (16-ounce) can black beans, drained

Sauté garlic in olive oil in skillet. Stir in squash, tomatoes, mushrooms, scallions and jalapeño peppers. Add soy sauce, salt and pepper; mix well. Bring to a boil; reduce heat. Simmer, covered, until vegetables are tender, stirring occasionally. Stir in black beans. Simmer until heated through, stirring occasionally. Drain any excess liquid. Serve over hot cooked saffron rice.

MUSHROOMS BAKED IN CREAM

Yield:
8 servings

*Approx Per
Serving:*
Cal 264
Prot 4 g
Carbo 7 g
T Fat 25 g
*85% Calories
from Fat*
Chol 66 mg
Fiber 1 g
Sod 342 mg

1 pound large
  mushrooms
1 tablespoon minced
  onion
1/4 cup butter
1/3 cup fine dry bread
  crumbs
1/2 teaspoon salt

1/4 teaspoon paprika
1/8 teaspoon pepper
3 to 5 slices bacon,
  finely chopped
1 cup whipping cream
1/2 teaspoon
  Worcestershire sauce

Remove stems from mushroom caps, reserving caps.
Chop stems finely. Simmer chopped stems and onion in
butter in skillet for 5 minutes, stirring gently. Stir in
bread crumbs, salt, paprika and pepper gently. Stuff
mushroom caps with mixture. Arrange in baking dish;
sprinkle with bacon. Pour mixture of cream and Worcestershire sauce around mushrooms. Bake at 400 degrees
for 15 to 20 minutes or until bacon is cooked through.

GOLDEN PARMESAN POTATOES

Yield:
12 servings

*Approx Per
Serving:*
Cal 149
Prot 3 g
Carbo 22 g
T Fat 6 g
*35% Calories
from Fat*
Chol 15 mg
Fiber 1 g
Sod 229 mg

1/4 cup sifted flour
1/4 cup grated Parmesan
  cheese
3/4 teaspoon salt
1/8 teaspoon pepper

6 large potatoes, peeled,
  cut into quarters
1/3 cup butter
Chopped fresh parsley

Mix flour, cheese, salt and pepper in food storage bag.
Rinse potatoes. Shake potatoes in flour mixture in bag
until coated. Melt butter in 9x13-inch baking pan. Arrange potatoes in single layer over butter. Bake at 375
degrees for 1 hour or until golden brown, turning 1 time.
Sprinkle with parsley. May be prepared and baked in
advance and reheated just before serving.

AU GRATIN POTATOES

Yield:
12 servings

Approx Per
Serving:
Cal 186
Prot 5 g
Carbo 23 g
T Fat 9 g
41% Calories
from Fat
Chol 24 mg
Fiber 1 g
Sod 240 mg

6 medium potatoes,
  peeled, sliced
1 small onion, finely
  chopped
3 tablespoons butter
3 tablespoons flour
1¹/₂ cups milk

³/₄ cup shredded
  Velveeta cheese
1 cup bread crumbs
Paprika to taste
2 tablespoons melted
  butter

Combine potatoes with enough water to cover in sauce-pan. Cook for 15 minutes or until tender; drain. Arrange in baking dish. Sauté onion in 3 tablespoons butter in skillet. Stir in flour until mixed. Add milk and cheese; mix well. Cook until cheese melts and sauce is thickened, stirring constantly. Pour over potatoes. Sprinkle with bread crumbs and paprika. Drizzle with 2 tablespoons butter. Bake at 350 degrees for 20 to 30 minutes or until bubbly and golden brown.

SMOTHERED POTATOES

Yield:
12 servings

Approx Per
Serving:
Cal 101
Prot 2 g
Carbo 19 g
T Fat 2 g
21% Calories
from Fat
Chol 0 mg
Fiber 1 g
Sod 59 mg

6 to 8 medium potatoes,
  peeled, sliced
2 tablespoons vegetable
  oil
1 large onion, chopped
¹/₂ green bell pepper,
  chopped

1 teaspoon garlic powder
1 teaspoon pepper
¹/₂ teaspoon seasoned salt
Red pepper flakes to
  taste
¹/₂ cup water

Cook potatoes in oil in skillet until tender-crisp; drain. Add onion, green pepper, garlic powder, pepper, seasoned salt, red pepper flakes and water; mix well. Simmer until potatoes are tender, adding additional water as needed. May add cooked pork sausage to mixture.

CREAMY SPINACH BAKE

Yield:
6 servings

Approx Per
Serving:
Cal 199
Prot 8 g
Carbo 7 g
T Fat 16 g
70% Calories
from Fat
Chol 34 mg
Fiber 2 g
Sod 377 mg

4 slices bacon
2 (10-ounce) packages
  frozen chopped
  spinach, thawed,
  drained

1¹/2 cups sour cream
1 envelope onion soup
  mix
¹/3 cup grated Parmesan
  cheese

Fry bacon until crisp; crumble. Combine spinach, sour cream and soup mix in bowl; mix well. Spoon into lightly greased 1-quart baking dish; sprinkle with cheese. Bake at 350 degrees for 30 minutes. Top with bacon. May substitute chopped broccoli for spinach.

SPINACH SOUFFLE DELUXE

Yield:
2 servings

Approx Per
Serving:
Cal 227
Prot 14 g
Carbo 8 g
T Fat 16 g
63% Calories
from Fat
Chol 243 mg
Fiber 1 g
Sod 623 mg

¹/2 cup chopped cooked
  spinach
1 tablespoon butter
2 teaspoons flour
¹/2 cup milk
¹/4 teaspoon salt

Pepper to taste
2 egg yolks, beaten
3 tablespoons grated
  Parmesan cheese
2 egg whites, stiffly
  beaten

Squeeze moisture from spinach. Melt butter in heavy saucepan. Stir in flour until smooth. Cook for 3 to 4 minutes or until bubbly, stirring constantly. Stir in milk. Cook over low heat for 6 to 8 minutes or until thickened, stirring constantly. Season with salt and pepper. Stir ¹/4 of the hot mixture into egg yolks; stir egg yolks into hot mixture. Add spinach and cheese; mix well. Fold in egg whites. Spoon into lightly greased 1-quart soufflé dish. Bake at 325 degrees for 40 to 50 minutes or until set. Serve immediately.

SQUASH CASSEROLE

Yield:
8 servings

Approx Per Serving:
Cal 322
Prot 5 g
Carbo 28 g
T Fat 22 g
60% Calories from Fat
Chol 13 mg
Fiber 1 g
Sod 825 mg

2 pounds squash, cooked, drained, mashed
1 (8-ounce) package corn bread stuffing
1 cup sour cream
1 (10-ounce) can cream of mushroom soup
1/4 cup margarine
1 carrot, grated
1 onion, chopped
Salt and pepper to taste
1/4 cup melted margarine

Combine squash, 1/2 of the stuffing, sour cream, soup, 1/4 cup margarine, carrot, onion, salt and pepper in bowl; mix well. May add a small amount of water as needed for desired consistency. Spoon into large baking dish. Sprinkle with mixture of 1/4 cup melted margarine and remaining stuffing. Bake at 350 degrees for 30 to 40 minutes or until brown. May be frozen before baked for future use.

FRIED GREEN TOMATOES

Yield:
8 servings

Approx Per Serving:
Cal 83
Prot 3 g
Carbo 14 g
T Fat 1 g
16% Calories from Fat
Chol 29 mg
Fiber 2 g
Sod 26 mg

1 egg
1/2 cup milk
1/2 cup cornmeal
1/4 cup flour
3 or 4 large firm green tomatoes, cut into 1/8- to 1/4-inch slices
Shortening for frying
Salt to taste

Beat egg and milk in bowl. Combine cornmeal and flour in bowl; mix well. Dip tomato slices in egg mixture; coat with cornmeal mixture. Fry in 1/2-inch deep heated shortening in heavy skillet until brown on both sides; drain. Sprinkle with salt.

Nutritional information does not include shortening for frying.

Spinach-Stuffed Tomatoes

Yield:
4 servings

Approx Per Serving:
Cal 127
Prot 8 g
Carbo 11 g
T Fat 7 g
46% Calories from Fat
Chol 16 mg
Fiber 3 g
Sod 455 mg

1 (10-ounce) package frozen chopped spinach, cooked, drained
4 small tomatoes
4 ounces jalapeño pepper cheese spread, cut into cubes
1/8 teaspoon onion powder
1/8 teaspoon garlic powder
1 1/2 tablespoons butter cracker crumbs
Paprika to taste

Squeeze spinach until barely moist. Slice top from each tomato; scoop out 1-inch of pulp. Discard pulp and tomato tops. Combine spinach, cheese, onion powder and garlic powder in saucepan. Cook until cheese melts, stirring constantly. Spoon into tomatoes. Place in 9x13-inch baking pan. Sprinkle with cracker crumbs and paprika. Bake at 300 degrees for 15 minutes or until heated through.

Sweet Potato Casserole

Yield:
12 servings

Approx Per Serving:
Cal 573
Prot 5 g
Carbo 83 g
T Fat 26 g
40% Calories from Fat
Chol 96 mg
Fiber 5 g
Sod 198 mg

6 to 8 medium sweet potatoes, cooked, peeled
1/2 cup butter, softened
2 cups sugar
3 eggs, beaten
1/2 cup milk
1 tablespoon vanilla extract
Orange juice to taste
1/2 cup butter
1/2 cup flour
1 cup packed light brown sugar
1 cup flaked coconut
1 cup chopped pecans

Mash sweet potatoes with 1/2 cup butter in bowl. Stir in sugar, eggs, milk, vanilla and orange juice. Spoon into baking pan. Melt 1/2 cup butter in saucepan. Remove from heat. Stir in flour and brown sugar until smooth. Add coconut and pecans; mix well. Sprinkle over prepared layer. Bake at 350 degrees for 1 hour.

COMPANY SWEET POTATO CASSEROLE

Yield:
8 servings

Approx Per
Serving:
Cal 579
Prot 6 g
Carbo 75 g
T Fat 30 g
46% Calories
from Fat
Chol 105 mg
Fiber 3 g
Sod 232 mg

3 cups mashed sweet
   potatoes
1 cup sugar
2 eggs, beaten
1 tablespoon vanilla
   extract
1/2 cup melted butter
1 cup packed brown
   sugar
1/2 cup flour
1/3 cup butter, softened
1 cup chopped walnuts

Combine sweet potatoes, sugar, eggs, vanilla and 1/2 cup butter in bowl; mix well. Spoon into buttered 1-quart baking dish. Combine brown sugar and flour in bowl; mix well. Cut in 1/3 cup butter until crumbly. Stir in walnuts. Sprinkle over prepared layer. Bake at 350 degrees for 30 minutes.

ZUCCHINI BOATS

Yield:
4 servings

Approx Per
Serving:
Cal 254
Prot 13 g
Carbo 22 g
T Fat 14 g
47% Calories
from Fat
Chol 28 mg
Fiber 4 g
Sod 333 mg

4 medium zucchini
1/4 cup chopped onion
1/2 teaspoon chopped
   garlic
1 tablespoon olive oil
1/2 cup bread crumbs
Salt and pepper to taste
1/4 to 1/2 cup shredded
   Cheddar cheese
1/4 cup bread crumbs
2 ounces Monterey Jack
   cheese, cut into 4 slices

Cut zucchini lengthwise into halves. Place cut side down in microwave-safe dish. Microwave, covered, until tender. Scoop out pulp and chop, reserving shells. Sauté onion and garlic in olive oil in skillet. Stir in chopped zucchini. Add 1/2 cup bread crumbs or just enough to thicken; mix well. Season with salt and pepper. Stir in Cheddar cheese. Cook until cheese melts, stirring constantly. Spoon into zucchini shells. Place in baking pan. Sprinkle with 1/4 cup bread crumbs. Top with Monterey Jack cheese. Bake at 350 degrees for 20 minutes or until brown and cheese melts.

Veggie Casserole

Yield:
6 servings

Approx Per
Serving:
Cal 499
Prot 9 g
Carbo 26 g
T Fat 41 g
73% Calories
from Fat
Chol 52 mg
Fiber 5 g
Sod 673 mg

1 (15-ounce) can
Veg-All, drained
1 cup shredded Cheddar
cheese
1 cup chopped Vidalia
onion
1 cup chopped celery

1 (8-ounce) can water
chestnuts, drained
1 cup mayonnaise
1 cup cracker crumbs
2 tablespoons melted
butter

Combine Veg-All, cheese, onion, celery and water chestnuts in bowl; mix well. Stir in mayonnaise. Spoon into baking dish sprayed with nonstick cooking spray. Sprinkle with mixture of cracker crumbs and butter. Bake at 350 degrees for 1 hour.

Turkey Dressing

Yield:
12 servings

Approx Per
Serving:
Cal 274
Prot 11 g
Carbo 44 g
T Fat 6 g
18% Calories
from Fat
Chol 120 mg
Fiber 4 g
Sod 901 mg

Turkey neck
1 tablespoon salt
1 large onion
3 stalks celery
4 cups water
3 cups cornmeal
1 cup flour
2 eggs, beaten
2 cups buttermilk

1 teaspoon sugar
1 (6-ounce) can
mushrooms, drained
1 (10-ounce) can cream
of mushroom soup
2 cups chopped celery
2 cups chopped onions
3 tablespoons sage
3 eggs, beaten

Combine turkey neck, salt, 1 onion, 3 stalks celery and water in stockpot. Cook for 1 hour or until turkey is tender. Drain, discarding onion and 3 stalks celery; reserve broth. Remove turkey from bone; chop. Combine cornmeal, flour, 2 eggs, buttermilk and sugar in bowl; mix well. Spoon into large baking pan. Bake in hot oven until brown and crisp; crumble. Combine turkey, crumbled corn bread, reserved broth, mushrooms, soup, 2 cups chopped celery, 2 cups chopped onions, sage and 3 eggs in bowl; mix well. Spoon into baking pan. Bake at 350 degrees for 45 to 60 minutes or until brown. May use 1 cup fresh mushrooms instead of canned mushrooms.

CHILIES RELLENOS CASSEROLE

Yield:
8 servings

Approx Per
Serving:
Cal 394
Prot 23 g
Carbo 14 g
T Fat 27 g
63% Calories
from Fat
Chol 230 mg
Fiber 1 g
Sod 966 mg

7 to 8 slices white
  bread, crusts trimmed
2 tablespoons butter,
  softened
2 cups shredded
  Cheddar cheese
2 cups shredded
  Monterey Jack cheese
1 (4-ounce) can diced
  green chilies, drained

6 eggs
2 cups milk
2 teaspoons paprika
1 teaspoon salt
1/2 teaspoon oregano
1/2 teaspoon pepper
1/4 teaspoon garlic
  powder
1/4 teaspoon dry mustard

Spread 1 side of bread slices with butter. Arrange bread butter side down in 8x12-inch baking dish. Layer Cheddar cheese, Monterey Jack cheese and chilies over bread. Beat eggs, milk, paprika, salt, oregano, pepper, garlic powder and dry mustard in mixer bowl until blended. Pour over prepared layers. Chill, covered, for 4 hours to overnight. Bake, uncovered, at 325 degrees for 50 minutes. Let stand for 10 minutes before serving.

GARLIC GRITS CASSEROLE

Yield:
4 servings

Approx Per
Serving:
Cal 407
Prot 16 g
Carbo 20 g
T Fat 30 g
65% Calories
from Fat
Chol 154 mg
Fiber 2 g
Sod 803 mg

1/2 cup quick-cooking
  grits
1 (6-ounce) roll garlic
  cheese, cut into cubes

1/4 cup melted margarine
2 eggs, slightly beaten
1 cup milk

Cook grits using package directions. Add cheese and margarine, stirring until cheese melts. Stir in mixture of eggs and milk. Spoon into lightly greased 1-quart baking dish. Bake at 350 degrees for 45 minutes or until set and golden brown.

LINGUINE WITH ANCHOVY SAUCE

Yield:
5 servings

Approx Per Serving:
Cal 645
Prot 22 g
Carbo 97 g
T Fat 20 g
27% Calories from Fat
Chol 15 mg
Fiber 8 g
Sod 910 mg

10 to 12 cloves of garlic, thinly sliced
5 to 6 tablespoons olive oil
1 (6-ounce) can tomato paste
1 tomato paste can water
1 (3-ounce) can flat anchovies
Pepper to taste
1¹/₂ tablespoons oregano
1 (16-ounce) package linguine, cooked, drained

Sauté garlic in olive oil in saucepan until light brown. Stir in tomato paste, water, anchovies, pepper and oregano. Cook for 45 minutes, stirring occasionally. Serve over hot cooked linguine.

MACARONI AND CHEESE

Yield:
40 servings

Approx Per Serving:
Cal 308
Prot 15 g
Carbo 20 g
T Fat 19 g
54% Calories from Fat
Chol 61 mg
Fiber 1 g
Sod 460 mg

24 ounces Velveeta cheese, cut into cubes
16 ounces sharp Cheddar cheese, cut into cubes
16 ounces mild Cheddar cheese, cut into cubes
3 (12-ounce) cans evaporated milk
¹/₂ cup margarine
2 (16-ounce) packages macaroni, cooked, drained, cooled
2 eggs, beaten
Pepper to taste
1 cup shredded Cheddar cheese

Combine Velveeta cheese, 16 ounces sharp Cheddar cheese, 16 ounces mild Cheddar cheese, evaporated milk and margarine in large saucepan. Cook over low heat until smooth, stirring frequently. Combine macaroni and eggs in bowl; mix well. Stir in cheese sauce; season with pepper. Spoon into 1 or 2 large baking pans; sprinkle with 1 cup shredded Cheddar cheese. Bake at 400 degrees for 35 to 40 minutes or until bubbly.

PENNE WITH STEAMED VEGETABLES

Yield:
4 servings

Approx Per Serving:
Cal 298
Prot 10 g
Carbo 55 g
T Fat 5 g
14% Calories from Fat
Chol 0 mg
Fiber 5 g
Sod 31 mg

1 cup broccoli flowerets
1 cup cauliflowerets
1 cup fresh green beans, trimmed, cut into 2-inch slices
1/2 cup sliced carrot
2 medium tomatoes, chopped
1/2 cup fresh corn kernels
1/4 cup chopped red onion
1 tablespoon olive oil
1/4 cup chopped fresh basil
Salt and freshly ground pepper to taste
8 ounces penne

Steam broccoli, cauliflower, sliced green beans and carrot in steamer for 5 minutes. Combine tomatoes, corn, red onion, olive oil, basil, salt and pepper in bowl; mix well. Combine penne and salt with enough water to cover in saucepan. Cook for 10 minutes or until al dente. Stir 1/4 cup of pasta cooking liquid into tomato mixture; drain pasta. Combine steamed vegetables, tomato mixture and pasta in bowl; mix well. Serve with grated Parmesan cheese.

BROWN RICE

Yield:
6 servings

Approx Per Serving:
Cal 210
Prot 5 g
Carbo 28 g
T Fat 9 g
37% Calories from Fat
Chol 0 mg
Fiber 1 g
Sod 864 mg

1 cup rice
1 (10-ounce) can beef bouillon
1 (10-ounce) can onion soup
1/4 cup margarine

Sprinkle rice in lightly greased 10x10-inch baking dish. Pour mixture of bouillon and onion soup over rice; do not stir. Dot with margarine. Bake, covered, at 350 degrees for 15 minutes; stir gently. Bake, covered, for 15 minutes.

DIRTY RICE

Yield:
8 servings

*Approx Per
Serving:*
Cal 293
Prot 19 g
Carbo 26 g
T Fat 12 g
*38% Calories
from Fat*
Chol 31 mg
Fiber <1 g
Sod 2375 mg

1 cup rice
1/2 cup melted butter
1 (10-ounce) can beef
   consommé

1 (10-ounce) can onion
  soup

Spread rice in 5x8-inch loaf pan. Pour mixture of butter, consommé and onion soup over rice; do not stir. Bake at 350 degrees for 1 hour. May add shrimp or meat to rice mixture.

Wild Rice with Almonds and Mushrooms

Sauté a 6-ounce package of wild rice, 8 ounces sliced fresh mushrooms, 2 tablespoons minced onion and 1/4 cup sliced almonds in 1/4 cup butter for 10 minutes or until almonds are golden brown. Stir in the rice seasoning packet and 2 1/4 cups boiling chicken broth. Pour into 1 1/2-quart baking dish and bake at 350 degrees for 40 minutes or until liquid is absorbed.

Scalloped Tomatoes

Layer sliced tomatoes alternately with mixture of bread crumbs, salt, pepper, melted butter and a small amount of sugar in baking dish, ending with bread crumb mixture. Bake in hot oven for 1 1/2 hours.

1900's Marker on Decatur's Square

Breads

ANGEL BISCUITS

Yield:
12 servings

Approx Per
Serving:
Cal 378
Prot 7 g
Carbo 47 g
T Fat 18 g
43% Calories
from Fat
Chol 1 mg
Fiber 2 g
Sod 373 mg

2 packages dry yeast
1/4 cup warm water
2 cups buttermilk
5 cups flour
1/4 cup sugar
1 tablespoon baking powder
1 teaspoon baking soda
1 teaspoon salt
1 cup shortening

Dissolve yeast in warm water. Let stand for 5 minutes. Stir in buttermilk. Set aside. Combine flour, sugar, baking powder, baking soda and salt in large bowl. Cut in shortening until crumbly. Add buttermilk mixture, stirring until dry ingredients are moistened. Knead dough on lightly floured surface 4 or 5 times. Roll dough 1/2 inch thick. Cut with 2 1/2-inch biscuit cutter. Place on lightly greased baking sheet. Let rise, covered, in warm place for 1 hour. Bake at 450 degrees for 10 to 12 minutes or until lightly browned. May make biscuits ahead of time and freeze until needed. Bake biscuits for 10 minutes and cool. Place in freezer bags. Store in freezer. To prepare for serving, place frozen biscuits on lightly greased baking sheet. Let stand until thawed. Bake at 450 degrees for 5 minutes or until heated through.

GARLIC CHEESE BISCUITS

Yield:
4 servings

Approx Per
Serving:
Cal 426
Prot 10 g
Carbo 38 g
T Fat 26 g
55% Calories
from Fat
Chol 21 mg
Fiber 1 g
Sod 965 mg

2 cups baking mix
2/3 cup milk
1/2 cup shredded Cheddar cheese
1/4 cup melted margarine
1/4 teaspoon garlic powder

Mix baking mix, milk and cheese in bowl until soft dough forms. Beat vigorously for 30 seconds. Drop by spoonfuls onto ungreased baking sheet. Bake in hot oven for 8 to 10 minutes or until golden brown. Mix margarine and garlic powder in small bowl. Brush over warm biscuits. Serve immediately.

GOOD SOUTHERN BISCUITS

Yield:
12 servings

*Approx Per
Serving:*
Cal 135
Prot 3 g
Carbo 17 g
T Fat 6 g
*41% Calories
from Fat*
Chol 1 mg
Fiber 1 g
Sod 341 mg

2 teaspoons
confectioners' sugar
2 teaspoons baking
powder

2 cups self-rising flour
1/3 cup shortening
1 cup buttermilk

Sift confectioners' sugar, baking powder and flour together in bowl. Cut in shortening until crumbly. Add buttermilk, stirring just until moistened. Roll dough 1/2 inch thick. Cut with biscuit cutter. Place on greased baking sheet. Bake at 450 degrees for 12 to 15 minutes or until golden brown.

CHEESY CORN BREAD

Yield:
8 servings

*Approx Per
Serving:*
Cal 431
Prot 10 g
Carbo 34 g
T Fat 29 g
*60% Calories
from Fat*
Chol 75 mg
Fiber 2 g
Sod 701 mg

1 1/2 cups cornmeal
3/4 cup vegetable oil
2 eggs
1 medium onion,
chopped
2 chopped green chilies
1 tablespoon baking
powder

1 (16-ounce) can
cream-style corn
1 teaspoon salt
1 1/2 cups shredded sharp
Cheddar cheese

Combine cornmeal, oil, eggs, onion, green chilies, baking powder, corn, salt and cheese in bowl; mix well. Pour into greased 9-inch baking dish. Bake at 350 degrees for 45 minutes.

COUNTRY CORN BREAD

Yield:
8 servings

Approx Per Serving:
Cal 234
Prot 5 g
Carbo 32 g
T Fat 10 g
37% Calories from Fat
Chol 33 mg
Fiber 2 g
Sod 521 mg

2 cups self-rising cornmeal
1¹/₄ to 1¹/₂ cups milk
¹/₄ cup vegetable oil
1 egg
2 tablespoons sugar
2 tablespoons fat-free mayonnaise-type salad dressing

Combine cornmeal, milk, oil, egg, sugar and salad dressing in bowl; mix well. Pour into greased 9-inch baking pan. Bake at 425 degrees for 25 to 30 minutes or until corn bread tests done. May substitute buttermilk for milk. May omit sugar.

SPIDER BREAD

Yield:
8 servings

Approx Per Serving:
Cal 194
Prot 6 g
Carbo 29 g
T Fat 6 g
28% Calories from Fat
Chol 67 mg
Fiber 1 g
Sod 391 mg

1 cup flour
¹/₂ cup plus 2 tablespoons yellow cornmeal
¹/₄ cup sugar
1 teaspoon baking soda
¹/₂ teaspoon baking powder
³/₄ teaspoon salt
2 eggs
1 cup plain yogurt
¹/₄ cup milk
2 tablespoons butter
¹/₄ cup plain yogurt
1 tablespoon milk

Sift flour, cornmeal, sugar, baking soda, baking powder and salt together in large bowl. Combine eggs, 1 cup yogurt and ¹/₄ cup milk in bowl; mix well. Stir into dry ingredients just until moistened. Melt butter in oven-proof skillet. Pour most of melted butter into batter, leaving enough to coat skillet. Stir batter just until combined. Spoon into skillet. Cook over low heat for 5 to 10 minutes. Combine remaining yogurt and milk in small bowl. Drizzle over partially cooked bread. Bake at 300 degrees for 30 to 35 minutes or until bread tests done. This sweet moist bread is a recipe used in colonial days.

Mexican Corn Bread

Yield:
8 servings

*Approx Per
Serving:*
Cal 416
Prot 9 g
Carbo 28 g
T Fat 31 g
*65% Calories
from Fat*
Chol 81 mg
Fiber 2 g
Sod 559 mg

1¹/₂ cups self-rising
  cornmeal
1 cup cream-style corn
¹/₂ cup finely chopped
  onion
2 tablespoons chopped
  green bell pepper

2 or 3 jalapeño peppers,
  chopped
²/₃ cup cooking oil
1 cup sour cream
1 or 2 eggs
1 cup shredded Cheddar
  cheese

Grease baking pan. Preheat pan in 450-degree oven. Combine cornmeal, corn, onion, green pepper, jalapeño peppers, oil, sour cream and egg in bowl; mix well. Pour half the batter into hot pan. Sprinkle with cheese. Pour remaining batter over top. Bake until golden brown.

Mexican Hush Puppies

Yield:
8 servings

*Approx Per
Serving:*
Cal 370
Prot 14 g
Carbo 56 g
T Fat 11 g
*25% Calories
from Fat*
Chol 104 mg
Fiber 3 g
Sod 1131 mg

2 cups self-rising
  cornmeal
1 cup self-rising flour
¹/₂ teaspoon salt
3 tablespoons sugar
3 eggs, beaten
¹/₂ cup milk
1 (17-ounce) can
  cream-style corn

1¹/₂ cups shredded
  Cheddar cheese
1 large onion, chopped
2 jalapeño peppers,
  seeded, chopped
Vegetable oil for frying

Combine cornmeal, flour, salt and sugar in bowl. Mix eggs and milk in small bowl. Add to dry ingredients, stirring just until moistened. Stir in corn, cheese, onion and peppers. Drop by rounded tablespoonfuls into hot oil 2 inches deep in small Dutch oven. Fry a few at a time until golden brown, turning 1 time. Drain hush puppies on paper towels.

Nutritional information does not include oil for frying.

Pecan Breakfast Loaf

Yield:
8 servings

Approx Per Serving:
Cal 425
Prot 4 g
Carbo 49 g
T Fat 25 g
51% Calories from Fat
Chol 13 mg
Fiber 1 g
Sod 597 mg

2 (8-count) cans crescent rolls
1/4 cup margarine, softened
1/2 cup sugar
1 teaspoon cinnamon
1/2 cup chopped pecans
2 tablespoons honey
1/4 cup confectioners' sugar
2 tablespoons butter
1 teaspoon vanilla extract
1/2 cup pecan pieces

Line 5x9-inch loaf pan with foil; coat with nonstick cooking spray. Set aside. Unroll crescent rolls. Cut through perforations but do not separate. Brush with softened margarine. Mix sugar, cinnamon and 1/2 cup chopped pecans. Sprinkle evenly over rolls. Roll up 8 crescent rolls. Cut each into halves, making 16 cone-shaped rolls. Line bottom of prepared pan with 8 cones to a side with points pointing to middle of pan. Roll up remaining 8 rolls. Place over first layer. Bake at 375 degrees for 35 to 40 minutes or until golden brown. Combine honey, confectioners' sugar, butter, vanilla and remaining pecan pieces in saucepan. Bring to a boil. Cook for 2 minutes, stirring constantly. Lift baked loaf out of pan. Do not invert. Pour glaze over top. Serve immediately.

Doughnut Balls

Yield:
30 servings

Approx Per Serving:
Cal 59
Prot 1 g
Carbo 8 g
T Fat 2 g
34% Calories from Fat
Chol 8 mg
Fiber <1 g
Sod 109 mg

2 cups sifted flour
1/3 cup sugar
1 tablespoon baking powder
1 teaspoon salt
1 teaspoon nutmeg
1/4 cup vegetable oil
3/4 cup milk
1 egg, well beaten
Vegetable oil for frying

Sift flour, sugar, baking powder, salt and nutmeg in bowl. Add 1/4 cup oil, milk and beaten egg. Stir with a fork until mixed thoroughly. Drop by teaspoonfuls into oil heated to 375 degrees in deep fryer. Fry a few at a time for 3 minutes or until golden brown; drain. May roll in cinnamon sugar or drizzle thin glaze over tops.

Nutritional information does not include oil for frying.

BANANA PINEAPPLE BREAD

Yield:
12 servings

Approx Per Serving:
Cal 146
Prot 3 g
Carbo 28 g
T Fat 3 g
17% Calories from Fat
Chol 0 mg
Fiber 2 g
Sod 124 mg

1¹/₂ cups all-purpose flour
³/₄ cup whole wheat flour
¹/₄ cup packed dark brown sugar
2 tablespoons wheat germ
1 tablespoon baking powder
¹/₂ teaspoon baking soda
¹/₄ teaspoon cinnamon
³/₄ cup mashed ripe banana
1 (8-ounce) can crushed pineapple, drained
2 tablespoons canola or corn oil
1 egg white

Combine all-purpose flour, whole wheat flour, brown sugar, wheat germ, baking powder, baking soda and cinnamon in large bowl. Mix banana, pineapple, oil and egg white in small bowl. Add to dry ingredients, stirring just until moistened. Pour into 5x9-inch loaf pan coated with nonstick cooking spray. Bake at 350 degrees for 50 to 55 minutes or until bread tests done. Cool in pan on wire rack for 10 minutes. Remove to wire rack to cool completely. May wrap cooled loaf in a double thickness of foil. Store in freezer for up to 3 months.

ONION CHEESE BREAD

Yield:
12 servings

Approx Per Serving:
Cal 127
Prot 5 g
Carbo 10 g
T Fat 8 g
53% Calories from Fat
Chol 29 mg
Fiber <1 g
Sod 250 mg

1 egg, beaten
¹/₂ cup milk
1 tablespoon vegetable oil
1¹/₂ cups baking mix
¹/₂ cup chopped onion
1 cup shredded sharp Cheddar cheese
1 tablespoon poppy seeds

Mix egg, milk and oil in bowl. Add baking mix, onion and cheese, stirring until mixed. Pour into greased 5x9-inch loaf pan. Sprinkle with poppy seeds. Bake at 350 degrees for 1 hour.

PUMPKIN BREAD

Yield:
12 servings

Approx Per
Serving:
Cal 617
Prot 6 g
Carbo 84 g
T Fat 30 g
43% Calories
from Fat
Chol 0 mg
Fiber 3 g
Sod 318 mg

3¹/2 cups flour
3 cups sugar
2 teaspoons baking soda
1 teaspoon cinnamon
1 teaspoon nutmeg
¹/2 teaspoon ground
cloves

1 teaspoon salt
2 cups pumpkin purée
1 cup vegetable oil
²/3 cup (about) water
1³/4 cups pecans

Combine flour, sugar, baking soda, cinnamon, nutmeg, cloves and salt in large bowl. Mix pumpkin, oil, water and pecans in bowl. Add to dry ingredients, stirring just until moistened. Pour into 2 greased loaf pans. Bake at 350 degrees for 50 minutes. May need to use less water if pumpkin purée is thin.

QUICK MUFFINS

Yield:
6 servings

Approx Per
Serving:
Cal 251
Prot 3 g
Carbo 17 g
T Fat 19 g
69% Calories
from Fat
Chol 9 mg
Fiber 1 g
Sod 453 mg

1 cup self-rising flour
¹/2 cup sour cream

¹/2 cup melted margarine

Mix flour, sour cream and melted margarine in bowl. Spoon into ungreased muffin cups. Bake at 350 degrees for 30 minutes.

SUNDAY MORNING MUFFINS

Yield:
15 servings

Approx Per Serving:
Cal 208
Prot 5 g
Carbo 34 g
T Fat 8 g
31% Calories from Fat
Chol 29 mg
Fiber 5 g
Sod 279 mg

2 (10-ounce) packages bran muffin mix
2/3 cup skim milk
2 eggs
1/4 cup honey
3/4 cup sliced almonds

Combine muffin mix, milk, eggs, honey and almonds in bowl. Stir just until moistened. Spoon 1/4 cup batter into each muffin cup coated with nonstick cooking spray. Bake at 400 degrees for 15 minutes. May add 1 cup blueberries to batter.

SANDI'S HOMEMADE PANCAKES

Yield:
10 servings

Approx Per Serving:
Cal 180
Prot 5 g
Carbo 22 g
T Fat 7 g
38% Calories from Fat
Chol 49 mg
Fiber 1 g
Sod 288 mg

2 cups less 2 tablespoons flour
2 tablespoons cornmeal
2 tablespoons baking powder
Salt to taste
2 eggs
2 cups milk
2 to 4 tablespoons melted margarine
1 teaspoon vanilla extract
Vegetable oil for frying

Combine flour, cornmeal, baking powder, salt, eggs, milk, margarine and vanilla in bowl; mix well. Pour batter into hot oil in griddle. Bake until brown on both sides, turning once. Serve hot with butter and syrup or fruit.

Nutritional information does not include oil for frying.

POPOVERS

Yield:
6 servings

*Approx Per
Serving:*
Cal 170
Prot 8 g
Carbo 19 g
T Fat 7 g
*37% Calories
from Fat*
Chol 152 mg
Fiber 1 g
Sod 437 mg

4 eggs
1 cup milk
1 tablespoon melted
  butter

1 cup flour
1 teaspoon sugar
1 teaspoon salt

Beat eggs in mixer bowl until light and fluffy. Add milk and melted butter; mix well. Combine flour, sugar and salt in bowl. Add to egg mixture; beat until smooth. Pour batter into 6 greased custard cups. Place cups on baking sheet. Bake at 400 degrees for 25 minutes. Reduce oven temperature to 350 degrees. Bake for 25 minutes longer. Turn off oven. Let popovers stand in oven for 5 to 10 minutes. May remove top third and fill with hot creamed chicken, seafood, cold chicken salad or shrimp salad to use as a main dish. Replace top, leaving it slightly atilt to reveal filling.

BUTTERMILK DINNER ROLLS

Yield:
16 servings

*Approx Per
Serving:*
Cal 185
Prot 6 g
Carbo 35 g
T Fat 2 g
*12% Calories
from Fat*
Chol 14 mg
Fiber 1 g
Sod 117 mg

2 packages dry yeast
$1/4$ cup warm
  (105-degree to
  115-degree) water
$1^3/4$ cups nonfat
  buttermilk

$1/4$ cup sugar
2 tablespoons
  margarine, softened
$1/2$ teaspoon salt
1 egg, lightly beaten
5 cups bread flour

Dissolve yeast in warm water. Let stand for 5 minutes. Combine with buttermilk, sugar, margarine, salt and egg in large mixer bowl. Beat at medium speed until well blended. Add 2 cups of the flour. Beat for 2 minutes. Stir in enough remaining flour to make a soft dough. Knead on floured surface for 8 to 10 minutes or until smooth and elastic. Place in bowl coated with nonstick cooking spray, turning to coat surface. Let rise, covered, in warm place for 45 minutes or until doubled in bulk. Punch dough down. Divide dough into halves. Divide each half into 8 portions. Shape each into a ball. Place 1 inch apart on baking sheet coated with nonstick cooking spray. Let rise, covered, for 30 minutes or until doubled in bulk. Bake at 325 degrees for 18 to 20 minutes or until light golden brown. Remove to wire rack to cool.

CHEESE BATTER BREAD

Yield:
12 servings

Approx Per Serving:
Cal 258
Prot 11 g
Carbo 21 g
T Fat 15 g
51% Calories from Fat
Chol 75 mg
Fiber 4 g
Sod 410 mg

³/4 cup warm milk or water
¹/4 cup unrefined vegetable oil
1 tablespoon raw honey
3 eggs, beaten
2¹/2 cups whole wheat flour

1 package dry yeast
1¹/2 teaspoons sea salt
¹/4 cup toasted sesame seeds
2 cups shredded Cheddar cheese
1 tablespoon sesame seeds

Combine milk, oil, honey and eggs in mixer bowl; mix well. Mix flour, yeast, salt, ¹/4 cup sesame seeds and cheese in bowl. Add to milk mixture. Beat for 3 to 4 minutes. Shape into loaf. Place in oiled 5x9-inch loaf pan. Let rise for 45 to 60 minutes. Press additional 1 tablespoon sesame seeds into top of loaf. Bake at 350 degrees for 45 minutes.

DILLY BREAD

Yield:
12 servings

Approx Per Serving:
Cal 137
Prot 5 g
Carbo 21 g
T Fat 3 g
22% Calories from Fat
Chol 26 mg
Fiber 1 g
Sod 291 mg

1 package dry yeast
¹/4 cup warm (110-degree) water
¹/4 teaspoon sugar
1 cup cream-style cottage cheese
2 tablespoons sugar
1 tablespoon minced onion

1 tablespoon butter
2 teaspoons dillseeds
1 teaspoon salt
1 egg
¹/4 teaspoon baking soda
2¹/4 cups flour
1 tablespoon butter
Coarse salt to taste

Dissolve yeast in warm water with ¹/4 teaspoon sugar. Combine next 8 ingredients in saucepan. Cook until heated through. Stir in yeast mixture. Add flour gradually until stiff dough is formed, mixing well after each addition. Place in greased bowl, turning to grease surface. Let rise, covered, in warm place for 1 hour or until doubled in bulk. Punch dough down. Place in greased 1¹/2-quart baking dish. Let rise, covered, for 30 to 40 minutes or until doubled in bulk. Bake at 350 degrees for 40 to 50 minutes or until bread tests done. Brush with remaining butter; sprinkle with coarse salt.

ONION BREAD

Yield:
24 servings

Approx Per
Serving:
Cal 128
Prot 4 g
Carbo 23 g
T Fat 3 g
18% Calories
from Fat
Chol 4 mg
Fiber <1 g
Sod 282 mg

1 package dry yeast
1/4 cup hot water
1 cup scalded milk
1 cup water
2 tablespoons butter

2 tablespoons sugar
1 tablespoon salt
6 cups unbleached flour
1/2 cup chives
1/4 cup poppy seeds

Dissolve yeast in 1/4 cup hot water in bowl. Let stand for 10 minutes. Combine scalded milk, 1 cup water, butter, sugar and salt in bowl; mix well. Stir in yeast mixture. Add 1 cup of the flour, chives and poppy seeds; mix well. Add flour 1 1/2 cups at a time just until dough no longer sticks to side of bowl, mixing well after each addition. Knead in remaining flour on floured surface until smooth and elastic. Shape into ball. Place in greased bowl, turning to grease surface. Let rise, covered, for 1 to 1 1/2 hours or until doubled in bulk. Punch dough down. Divide into halves; shape into loaves. Place in greased 5x9-inch loaf pans. Bake at 425 degrees for 15 minutes. Reduce temperature to 350 degrees. Bake for 25 to 30 minutes longer.

WHOLE WHEAT BREAD

Yield:
36 servings

Approx Per
Serving:
Cal 179
Prot 5 g
Carbo 34 g
T Fat 3 g
16% Calories
from Fat
Chol 7 mg
Fiber 4 g
Sod 266 mg

2 packages dry yeast
1/2 cup warm water
1 teaspoon sugar
1/4 teaspoon ginger
2 1/2 cups warm water
4 teaspoons salt

3/4 cup packed brown
   sugar
4 cups all-purpose flour
1/2 cup butter
1 cup boiling water
8 cups whole wheat flour

Dissolve yeast in 1/2 cup warm water with sugar and ginger in small bowl. Combine 2 1/2 cups warm water, salt, brown sugar and 2 cups of the all-purpose flour in large bowl; mix well. Add yeast mixture; mix well. Let rise, covered, in warm place for 1 1/2 to 2 hours. Melt butter in boiling water in bowl. Let stand until cool. Add whole wheat flour; mix well. Stir into yeast mixture. Add remaining all-purpose flour; mix well. Knead on floured surface. Place in greased bowl, turning to grease surface. Let rise, covered, for 45 minutes. Shape into 3 loaves. Place in 5x9-inch loaf pans. Let rise, covered, for 30 minutes. Bake at 375 degrees for 35 minutes.

Governors Mansion

~

Desserts

APPLE CRISP

Yield:
12 servings

Approx Per Serving:
Cal 421
Prot 2 g
Carbo 61 g
T Fat 19 g
41% Calories from Fat
Chol 41 mg
Fiber 1 g
Sod 200 mg

2 (21-ounce) cans apple pie filling
Cinnamon to taste
Sugar to taste
1/2 cup butter
1 (2-layer) package butter cake mix
1/2 cup butter

Spread pie filling in 9x12-inch baking dish. Sprinkle with cinnamon and sugar; dot with 1/2 cup butter. Spread cake mix evenly over layers. Dot with 1/2 cup butter. Bake at 350 degrees for 1 hour.

APPLE AND RAISIN CRISP

Yield:
6 servings

Approx Per Serving:
Cal 217
Prot 1 g
Carbo 47 g
T Fat 5 g
18% Calories from Fat
Chol 11 mg
Fiber 4 g
Sod 34 mg

3/4 cup fresh whole wheat or white bread crumbs
1/4 cup packed dark brown sugar
3/4 teaspoon cinnamon
1/4 teaspoon allspice
6 large Granny Smith apples, peeled, cut into 1/2-inch slices
1/2 cup raisins
1 tablespoon fresh lemon juice
1/3 cup apple cider or water
2 tablespoons unsalted butter, chilled, chopped

Combine bread crumbs, brown sugar, cinnamon and allspice in bowl; mix well. Combine apples and raisins in bowl; mix well. Add lemon juice, tossing to coat. Spread 1/2 of the apple mixture in 2 1/2-quart baking dish sprayed with nonstick cooking spray. Pour apple cider over top. Dot with 1/2 of the butter and sprinkle with 1/2 of the bread crumb mixture. Layer remaining apple mixture, butter and remaining bread crumb mixture over prepared layers. Bake at 375 degrees for 30 to 35 minutes or until bubbly and brown. Remove to wire rack to cool. Serve warm or chilled.

APPLE DUMP CAKE

Yield:
8 servings

Approx Per
Serving:
Cal 686
Prot 4 g
Carbo 82 g
T Fat 39 g
51% Calories
from Fat
Chol 62 mg
Fiber 2 g
Sod 657 mg

1 (16-ounce) can sliced
  apples
3/4 cup packed brown
  sugar

1 (2-layer) package spice
  cake mix
1 cup butter
1 cup chopped pecans

Arrange apples in greased baking dish. Sprinkle with brown sugar and cake mix. Dot with butter; sprinkle with pecans. Bake at 350 degrees for 1 hour or until brown and bubbly.

BANANA AND PINEAPPLE DESSERT

Yield:
15 servings

Approx Per
Serving:
Cal 384
Prot 5 g
Carbo 45 g
T Fat 22 g
50% Calories
from Fat
Chol 24 mg
Fiber 2 g
Sod 415 mg

1 1/2 cups graham
  cracker crumbs
1/4 cup sugar
1/3 cup margarine,
  softened
3 bananas, sliced
8 ounces cream cheese,
  softened
3 1/2 cups milk

2 (4-ounce) packages
  vanilla instant
  pudding mix
1 (20-ounce) can
  crushed pineapple,
  drained
8 ounces whipped
  topping
1 cup chopped pecans

Combine graham cracker crumbs, sugar and margarine in bowl; mix well. Press evenly over bottom of 9x13-inch baking pan. Arrange sliced bananas over crumb layer. Whisk cream cheese in bowl until smooth. Add milk gradually, beating until smooth. Add pudding mix; mix well. Spread evenly over bananas. Spoon pineapple over prepared layers. Spread with whipped topping; sprinkle with pecans. Chill for 3 hours or longer.

LIGHT AMBROSIA CHEESECAKE

Yield:
12 servings

*Approx Per
Serving:*
Cal 161
Prot 5 g
Carbo 22 g
T Fat 6 g
*33% Calories
from Fat*
Chol 11 mg
Fiber 1 g
Sod 120 mg

3/4 cup Zwieback crumbs
1/4 cup flaked coconut,
   toasted
2 tablespoons melted
   light margarine
1 cup unsweetened
   pineapple juice
1 (3-ounce) package
   lemon gelatin
8 ounces light cream
   cheese, softened

1 1/2 cups fat-free sour
   cream
1/4 teaspoon coconut
   extract
1 (8-ounce) can
   juice-pack crushed
   pineapple
2 teaspoons cornstarch
1/4 cup flaked coconut,
   toasted

Combine Zwieback crumbs, 1/4 cup coconut and margarine in bowl; mix well. Press in bottom of 8-inch springform pan. Chill for 1 hour. Bring pineapple juice to a boil in saucepan. Remove from heat. Stir in gelatin until dissolved. Cool to lukewarm. Beat cream cheese and sour cream at high speed in mixer bowl until smooth. Add coconut extract and gelatin mixture, beating until blended. Spoon evenly over prepared layer. Chill, covered with plastic wrap, for 3 hours. Bring pineapple and cornstarch to a boil in saucepan, stirring occasionally. Boil for 3 minutes or until thickened, stirring constantly. Cool. Remove side of springform pan; place cheesecake on serving plate. Spread pineapple mixture over top; sprinkle outside edge with 1/4 cup coconut.

Cheese Danish

Pat an 8-count package of refrigerator crescent roll dough into a greased 9x13-inch baking pan, sealing edges and perforations. Spread with a mixture of 16 ounces cream cheese, 1 egg yolk, 1 cup sugar, 1 teaspoon lemon juice and 1 teaspoon vanilla. Top with another package of roll dough and bake at 375 degrees for 30 minutes.

BEST-EVER CHEESECAKE

Yield:
12 servings

Approx Per
Serving:
Cal 709
Prot 13 g
Carbo 52 g
T Fat 51 g
64% Calories
from Fat
Chol 253 mg
Fiber 1 g
Sod 490 mg

2 cups graham cracker
  crumbs
2 tablespoons sugar
1/2 cup melted butter
32 ounces cream cheese,
  softened

1³/4 cups sugar
7 eggs
3 cups sour cream
1 tablespoon plus 1
  teaspoon vanilla
  extract

Combine graham cracker crumbs, 2 tablespoons sugar and butter in bowl; mix well. Pat into bottom of greased 9-inch springform pan. Chill. Beat cream cheese in mixer bowl until light and fluffy. Add 1³/4 cups sugar gradually, beating until blended. Add eggs 1 at a time, beating well after each addition. Stir in sour cream and vanilla. Spoon into prepared pan. Bake at 350 degrees for 65 minutes. Turn off oven. Let stand in oven with door closed for 4 hours. Chill, loosely covered, for 12 hours.

CHERRY-TOPPED CHEESECAKE

Yield:
12 servings

Approx Per
Serving:
Cal 534
Prot 8 g
Carbo 73 g
T Fat 24 g
40% Calories
from Fat
Chol 117 mg
Fiber 1 g
Sod 478 mg

1 (2-layer) package
  yellow cake mix
2 tablespoons vegetable
  oil
1 egg, beaten
16 ounces cream cheese,
  softened
1/2 cup sugar

3 eggs
1¹/2 cups milk
3 tablespoons lemon
  juice
1 tablespoon vanilla
  extract
2 (21-ounce) cans cherry
  pie filling

Reserve 1 cup of the cake mix. Combine remaining cake mix, oil and 1 egg in bowl; mix well. Press evenly over bottom and ³/4 way up sides of greased 9x13-inch baking pan. Combine cream cheese, sugar, 3 eggs and reserved cake mix in mixer bowl. Beat at medium speed for 1 minute. Add milk, lemon juice and vanilla gradually, beating constantly at low speed until smooth. Spread over prepared layer. Bake at 300 degrees for 45 to 55 minutes or until set. Cool. Spread with cherry pie filling. Chill until serving time.

CHOCOLATE TURTLE CHEESECAKE

Yield:
10 servings

Approx Per Serving:
Cal 868
Prot 11 g
Carbo 85 g
T Fat 58 g
58% Calories from Fat
Chol 126 mg
Fiber 3 g
Sod 450 mg

2 cups vanilla wafer crumbs
6 tablespoons melted margarine
1 (14-ounce) package caramels
1 (5-ounce) can evaporated milk
1 cup chopped pecans, toasted
16 ounces cream cheese, softened
1/2 cup sugar
1 teaspoon vanilla extract
2 eggs
1/2 cup semisweet chocolate chips, melted
1 cup packed brown sugar
1/4 cup melted butter
2 tablespoons whipping cream
11/2 cups pecans halves

Combine vanilla wafer crumbs and margarine in bowl; mix well. Press evenly over bottom and side of 9-inch springform pan. Bake at 350 degrees for 10 minutes. Combine caramels and evaporated milk in saucepan. Cook over low heat until caramels melt, stirring frequently. Pour over baked layer; sprinkle with 1 cup chopped pecans. Combine cream cheese, sugar and vanilla in mixer bowl. Beat at medium speed until blended. Add eggs 1 at a time, beating well after each addition. Add melted chocolate; mix well. Pour over pecans. Bake at 450 degrees for 10 minutes. Reduce temperature to 250-degrees. Bake for 40 minutes. Loosen side of pan. Cool. Remove side of pan. Chill. Combine brown sugar, butter and whipping cream in bowl; mix well. Cool slightly. Spoon over chilled cheesecake. Arrange 11/2 cups pecan halves around edge of cheesecake. Garnish with whipped cream, chopped pecans or maraschino cherries.

Lime Curd

Beat 10 egg yolks with 1/2 cup sugar, zest of 6 limes and 3/4 cup fresh lime juice in a heavy saucepan. Bring just to the boiling point over low heat, whisking constantly. Remove from heat; stir in 1/2 cup unsalted butter until smooth and chill thoroughly. Whip 1 cup whipping cream, adding 1/2 cup sugar, 1 tablespoon at a time. Fold into chilled lime mixture and spoon into parfait glasses. Serve with toasted meringue or other light cookies and garnish with lime curls or mint sprigs.

CHERRY CHEESECAKE

Yield:
16 servings

**Approx Per
Serving:**
*Cal 441
Prot 6 g
Carbo 50 g
T Fat 25 g
50% Calories
from Fat
Chol 95 mg
Fiber 1 g
Sod 379 mg*

1 (2-layer) package
super moist yellow
cake mix
1/3 cup butter, softened
1 egg, beaten
2 teaspoons vanilla
extract
16 ounces cream cheese,
softened

3/4 cup sugar
2 eggs
1/4 cup sugar
2 cups sour cream
1 tablespoon vanilla
extract
1 (21-ounce) can cherry
pie filling

Combine cake mix, butter and 1 egg in mixer bowl. Beat at low speed until crumbly. Press into ungreased 9x13-inch baking pan. Beat 2 teaspoons vanilla, cream cheese, 3/4 cup sugar and 2 eggs in mixer bowl until light and fluffy. Spread over prepared layer. Bake at 350 degrees for 20 to 25 minutes or until set. Spread with mixture of next 3 ingredients. Cool. Spread with cherry pie filling. Chill, covered, for 8 hours or longer.

CREAMY CHEESECAKE

Yield:
12 servings

**Approx Per
Serving:**
*Cal 595
Prot 12 g
Carbo 45 g
T Fat 42 g
62% Calories
from Fat
Chol 257 mg
Fiber <1 g
Sod 419 mg*

1 1/2 cups graham
cracker crumbs
2 tablespoons melted
butter
2 teaspoons sugar
40 ounces cream cheese,
softened
1 tablespoon flour

1 3/4 cups sugar
1 tablespoon lemon juice
1 tablespoon vanilla
extract
5 eggs
3 egg yolks
1/4 cup whipping cream

Combine graham cracker crumbs, butter and 2 teaspoons sugar in bowl; mix well. Press into bottom of 10-inch springform pan. Beat cream cheese in mixer bowl in small amounts until light and fluffy. Add flour, beating until blended. Add 1 3/4 cups sugar gradually; mix well. Beat in lemon juice and vanilla until smooth. Add eggs and egg yolks 1 at a time, beating well after each addition. Stir in whipping cream. Spread over prepared layer. Bake at 500 degrees for 12 minutes. Reduce temperature to 200 degrees. Bake for 40 to 50 minutes. Let stand in oven with door closed overnight.

COTTAGE CHEESE CHEESECAKE

Yield:
12 servings

Approx Per Serving:
Cal 395
Prot 9 g
Carbo 33 g
T Fat 26 g
59% Calories from Fat
Chol 106 mg
Fiber 1 g
Sod 361 mg

1¹/₂ cups fine graham cracker crumbs
¹/₃ cup melted margarine
¹/₄ cup sugar
1 cup creamy cottage cheese
16 ounces cream cheese, softened

³/₄ cup sugar
2 tablespoons flour
2 teaspoons vanilla extract
3 eggs
¹/₄ cup milk
1 cup sour cream
1 cup sliced strawberries

Mix cracker crumbs, margarine and ¹/₄ cup sugar in bowl. Press evenly over bottom and 1³/₄ inches up side of 9-inch springform pan. Place on baking sheet. Beat cottage cheese in mixer bowl until almost smooth. Add next 4 ingredients. Beat until smooth, scraping bowl occasionally. Add eggs. Beat at low speed just until mixed. Stir in milk. Spoon into prepared pan. Bake at 350 degrees for 50 to 60 minutes or until set. Cool on wire rack for 5 to 10 minutes. Spread with sour cream. Cool for 30 minutes. Chill. Top with strawberries.

LEMON CHIP CHEESECAKE

Yield:
8 servings

Approx Per Serving:
Cal 430
Prot 6 g
Carbo 38 g
T Fat 29 g
60% Calories from Fat
Chol 111 mg
Fiber 1 g
Sod 366 mg

1 cup graham cracker crumbs
2 tablespoons margarine, softened
8 ounces cream cheese, softened
¹/₂ cup margarine, softened

³/₄ cup sugar
3 eggs
2 teaspoons grated lemon rind
1 teaspoon lemon extract
¹/₄ cup flour
¹/₄ cup miniature semi-sweet chocolate chips

Mix cracker crumbs and 2 tablespoons margarine in bowl. Press in 8x8-inch baking pan sprayed with nonstick cooking spray. Beat cream cheese and ¹/₂ cup margarine in mixer bowl at high speed until smooth. Beat in sugar until blended. Beat in eggs 1 at a time. Stir in lemon rind and lemon extract. Stir in flour and chocolate chips gradually. Spread over prepared layer. Bake at 300 degrees for 1 hour or until set. Cool on wire rack for 30 minutes. Chill for 6 hours. Garnish with additional chocolate chips.

New York Restaurant Cheesecake

Yield:
10 servings

Approx Per Serving:
Cal 583
Prot 10 g
Carbo 47 g
T Fat 40 g
60% Calories from Fat
Chol 197 mg
Fiber <1 g
Sod 413 mg

1/4 cup melted butter
1 cup graham cracker crumbs
32 ounces cream cheese, softened
1 3/4 cups sugar
4 eggs
1 teaspoon vanilla extract
3 tablespoons Cointreau or orange juice

Combine butter and graham cracker crumbs in bowl; mix well. Press into bottom of greased aluminum 3x8-inch pan. Beat cream cheese, sugar, eggs, vanilla and 2 tablespoons of the Cointreau in mixer bowl until smooth and creamy. Spoon over prepared layer. Drizzle with remaining Cointreau. Place in large baking pan with boiling water to reach halfway up side of cheesecake pan. Bake at 325 degrees for 1 1/2 to 2 hours or until set. Let stand in oven with door closed for 20 minutes. Remove to wire rack to cool. Invert onto serving platter. Chill, covered, until serving time. May freeze for future use. May substitute crumbled prepared graham cracker pie shell for graham cracker crumbs and butter.

Pineapple Cheesecake

Yield:
15 servings

Approx Per Serving:
Cal 311
Prot 5 g
Carbo 23 g
T Fat 22 g
63% Calories from Fat
Chol 98 mg
Fiber <1 g
Sod 222 mg

1 1/2 cups graham cracker crumbs
1/4 cup sugar
1/4 cup melted butter
16 ounces cream cheese, softened
1/4 cup sugar
3 eggs
1/2 teaspoon vanilla extract
1 (8-ounce) can crushed pineapple, drained
2 cups sour cream
1/4 cup sugar
1 teaspoon vanilla extract

Combine graham cracker crumbs, 1/4 cup sugar and butter in bowl; mix well. Reserve 1/4 of the mixture. Press remaining crumb mixture into 8x12-inch baking pan. Beat cream cheese and 1/4 cup sugar in mixer bowl until light and fluffy. Add eggs and 1/2 teaspoon vanilla, beating until smooth. Spoon into prepared pan. Bake at 350 degrees for 30 minutes. Spread pineapple evenly over cheesecake. Top with mixture of sour cream, 1/4 cup sugar and 1 teaspoon vanilla; sprinkle with reserved crumb mixture. Bake at 450 degrees for 10 minutes.

QUICK CHEESECAKES

Yield:
12 servings

Approx Per
Serving:
Cal 648
Prot 10 g
Carbo 57 g
T Fat 43 g
59% Calories
from Fat
Chol 150 mg
Fiber 1 g
Sod 518 mg

24 ounces cream cheese, softened
1 cup sugar
4 eggs
1 tablespoon vanilla extract

2 (9-inch) graham cracker pie shells
2 cups sour cream
1 tablespoon vanilla extract
1 tablespoon sugar

Combine cream cheese and 1 cup sugar in mixer bowl. Beat at low speed until blended. Add eggs 1 at a time, beating well after each addition. Beat in 1 tablespoon vanilla. Spoon into pie shells. Bake at 350 degrees for 35 minutes. Spread with mixture of sour cream, 1 tablespoon vanilla and 1 tablespoon sugar. Bake for 5 minutes. May substitute one 21-ounce can fruit pie filling for sour cream mixture.

CANNOLI CREAM

Yield:
4 servings

Approx Per
Serving:
Cal 318
Prot 10 g
Carbo 39 g
T Fat 15 g
39% Calories
from Fat
Chol 39 mg
Fiber 5 g
Sod 82 mg

1¼ cups ricotta cheese
⅓ cup orange marmalade
2 (1-ounce) bars semisweet chocolate, finely chopped

1 tablespoon Grand Marnier
¼ teaspoon vanilla extract
4 cups fresh strawberries

Process ricotta cheese in food processor for 2 minutes or until smooth. Add marmalade. Process until blended. Combine ricotta cheese mixture with chocolate, Grand Marnier and vanilla in bowl; mix well. Chill, covered, for 1 hour or longer. Spoon over strawberries in individual dessert bowls or goblets. May substitute blueberries or raspberries for strawberries.

PIZZA RICOTTA

Yield:
12 servings

Approx Per
Serving:
Cal 443
Prot 20 g
Carbo 35 g
T Fat 25 g
50% Calories
from Fat
Chol 269 mg
Fiber <1 g
Sod 240 mg

1 unbaked (9-inch) pie
  shell, thawed
48 ounces ricotta cheese
Juice of 2 lemons
1 1/4 cups sugar
12 eggs, beaten
1 teaspoon anise extract
1/4 cup confectioners'
  sugar

Line bottom of ungreased 9-inch springform pan with pie shell. Beat ricotta cheese, lemon juice and sugar in mixer bowl until smooth and creamy. Stir in eggs. Add anise extract; mix well. Spoon over prepared layer. Bake at 350 degrees for 1 1/4 to 1 1/2 hours or until set. Remove to wire rack to cool. Chill until serving time. Sprinkle with confectioners' sugar just before serving.

CHOCOLATE DUMP CAKE

Yield:
15 servings

Approx Per
Serving:
Cal 409
Prot 3 g
Carbo 48 g
T Fat 24 g
52% Calories
from Fat
Chol 0 mg
Fiber 2 g
Sod 446 mg

1 cup chocolate chips
1 (21-ounce) can cherry
  pie filling
1 (2-layer) package
  devil's food cake mix
1 cup margarine
1 cup chopped pecans

Layer chocolate chips, cherry pie filling, cake mix, margarine and nuts in order listed in greased baking pan. Bake at 350 degrees for 1 hour or until golden brown.

TRIPLE CHOCOLATE MESS

Yield:
8 servings

Approx Per Serving:
Cal 766
Prot 10 g
Carbo 75 g
T Fat 52 g
58% Calories from Fat
Chol 132 mg
Fiber 3 g
Sod 793 mg

1 (2-layer) package chocolate cake mix
2 cups sour cream
1 (4-ounce) package chocolate instant pudding mix
1 cup chocolate chips
3/4 cup vegetable oil
4 eggs, beaten
1 cup water

Combine cake mix, sour cream, pudding mix, chocolate chips, oil, eggs and water in bowl; mix well. Pour into slow cooker sprayed with nonstick cooking spray. Cook on Low for 6 hours. Spoon into dessert bowls. Serve with vanilla ice cream.

WHITE CHOCOLATE MOUSSE TORTE

Yield:
16 servings

Approx Per Serving:
Cal 538
Prot 7 g
Carbo 43 g
T Fat 38 g
63% Calories from Fat
Chol 87 mg
Fiber 0 g
Sod 159 mg

2 (6-ounce) packages chocolate-laced pirouette cookies
2 (10-ounce) packages vanilla milk chips
1/4 cup honey
16 ounces cream cheese, softened
1/4 to 1/3 cup Amaretto
2 cups whipping cream, whipped

Trim 1 edge of each cookie with serrated knife, reserving trimmed edges. Arrange enough cookies cut side down to go around outer edge of 8-inch springform pan. Crush reserved cookie pieces and remaining cookies. Sprinkle crumbs over bottom of pan. Heat vanilla chips in saucepan until melted, stirring frequently. Stir in honey. Beat in cream cheese and Amaretto with electric mixer until smooth. Fold in whipped cream. Spread over prepared layer. Chill, covered, for 4 hours to overnight. Garnish with chocolate curls. May substitute Kahlua, Bailey's Irish Creme, Frangelico or peppermint schnapps for Amaretto. Use 1/3 cup of mild-flavored liqueurs and 1/4 cup of stronger-flavored liqueurs.

DIRT CAKE

Yield:
12 servings

**Approx Per
Serving:**
*Cal 565
Prot 6 g
Carbo 71 g
T Fat 30 g
46% Calories
from Fat
Chol 31 mg
Fiber 1 g
Sod 700 mg*

8 ounces cream cheese,
 softened
1/4 cup margarine,
 softened
1 cup confectioners'
 sugar
2 (4-ounce) packages
 French vanilla instant
 pudding mix
3 1/2 cups milk
12 ounces whipped
 topping
1 (20-ounce) package
 chocolate sandwich
 cookies, crushed

Beat cream cheese, margarine and confectioners' sugar
in mixer bowl until smooth. Combine pudding mix and
milk in bowl; mix well. Add whipped topping; mix well.
Fold into cream cheese mixture. Alternate layers of cookie
crumbs and cream cheese mixture in bowl until all ingredients are used, starting and ending with cookie
crumbs. Decorate with silk flowers and gummy worms.

HOMEMADE ICE CREAM

Yield:
16 servings

**Approx Per
Serving:**
*Cal 388
Prot 16 g
Carbo 45 g
T Fat 17 g
38% Calories
from Fat
Chol 67 mg
Fiber 0 g
Sod 242 mg*

2 (14-ounce) cans
 sweetened condensed
 milk
2 quarts milk
2 tablespoons vanilla
 extract
1 gallon milk

Combine condensed milk, 2 quarts milk and vanilla in
large bowl, stirring until blended. Pour into 1-gallon ice
cream freezer container. Add 1 gallon milk or enough to
measure to fill line. Freeze using manufacturer's instructions. May add chocolate and fresh fruit if desired.

PEACH ICE CREAM

Yield:
16 servings

Approx Per Serving:
Cal 260
Prot 7 g
Carbo 45 g
T Fat 7 g
22% Calories from Fat
Chol 74 mg
Fiber 1 g
Sod 158 mg

4 egg yolks
1/2 teaspoon salt
2 1/2 cups sugar
1 teaspoon vanilla extract
2 (12-ounce) cans evaporated milk
4 egg whites, stiffly beaten
6 very ripe peaches, chopped or mashed
1 evaporated milk can water
1 (12-ounce) can apricot nectar
1 quart milk

Beat egg yolks in mixer bowl until lemon-colored. Add salt, sugar and vanilla; mix well. Add evaporated milk. Beat for 1 minute. Add egg whites; mix well. Stir in peaches, water, apricot nectar and milk. Pour into 1-gallon ice cream freezer container. Freeze using manufacturer's instructions.

TUTTI FRUTTI ICE CREAM

Yield:
16 servings

Approx Per Serving:
Cal 428
Prot 7 g
Carbo 64 g
T Fat 17 g
35% Calories from Fat
Chol 66 mg
Fiber 1 g
Sod 103 mg

1 (4-ounce) jar maraschino cherries
1 (8-ounce) can crushed pineapple
10 fresh peaches, mashed
1 large banana, mashed
2 cups whipping cream
1 (14-ounce) can sweetened condensed milk
2 1/2 cups sugar
2 quarts milk

Drain cherries, reserving liquid. Chop cherries. Combine cherries, cherry juice, undrained pineapple, peaches, banana, whipping cream, condensed milk, sugar and milk in large bowl; mix well. Pour into ice cream freezer container. Freeze using manufacturer's instructions.

AMERICA'S BEST PEACH COBBLER

Yield:
15 servings

**Approx Per
Serving:**
Cal 219
Prot 2 g
Carbo 41 g
T Fat 6 g
24% Calories
from Fat
Chol 29 mg
Fiber 1 g
Sod 190 mg

1 cup sugar
3 tablespoons flour
1/4 teaspoon cinnamon
Salt to taste
5 cups sliced fresh
  peaches
2 tablespoons butter
1 cup flour

1 cup sugar
1 teaspoon baking
  powder
3/4 teaspoon salt
1 egg, beaten
1/3 cup melted butter
Cinnamon to taste

Combine 1 cup sugar, 3 tablespoons flour, 1/4 teaspoon cinnamon and salt to taste in bowl; mix well. Stir in peaches gently. Spoon into ungreased 9x13-inch baking pan. Dot with 2 tablespoons butter. Combine 1 cup flour, 1 cup sugar, baking powder and 3/4 teaspoon salt in bowl; mix well. Add egg; mix well. Sprinkle evenly over prepared layer. Drizzle with 1/3 cup melted butter; sprinkle with cinnamon to taste. Bake at 350 degrees for 35 to 40 minutes or until brown. Serve with whipped cream or vanilla ice cream.

PEACH CUSTARD CAKE

Yield:
9 servings

**Approx Per
Serving:**
Cal 322
Prot 5 g
Carbo 48 g
T Fat 13 g
36% Calories
from Fat
Chol 59 mg
Fiber 1 g
Sod 265 mg

1 (29-ounce) can sliced
  peaches
1 1/2 cups flour
1/2 teaspoon salt
1/2 cup butter, softened

1/2 cup sugar
1/2 teaspoon cinnamon
1 egg, slightly beaten
1 cup evaporated milk

Drain peaches, reserving 1/2 cup syrup. Combine flour and salt in bowl; mix well. Cut in butter with pastry blender until crumbly. Pat evenly over bottom and halfway up sides of buttered 8x8-inch baking pan. Arrange peaches evenly over prepared layer. Sprinkle with mixture of sugar and cinnamon. Bake at 375 degrees for 20 minutes. Combine reserved peach syrup, egg and evaporated milk in bowl; mix well. Pour over baked layers. Bake for 30 minutes or until set. Serve warm or cold.

FRIED PEACHES

Yield:
10 servings

Approx Per Serving:
Cal 72
Prot <1 g
Carbo 19 g
T Fat <1 g
1% Calories from Fat
Chol 0 mg
Fiber 2 g
Sod 1 mg

Bacon drippings for frying
5 peaches, cut into halves
3 tablespoons cinnamon
$^1/_2$ cup plus 2 tablespoons sugar
$^1/_4$ cup water

Add just enough bacon drippings to 10-inch skillet to coat bottom. Fry peaches cut side down in drippings for 2 minutes. Turn peach halves. Fill centers with mixture of cinnamon and sugar. Pour water around peach halves. Cook, covered, for 3 minutes. Serve for breakfast with bacon and toast.

Nutritional information does not include bacon drippings for frying.

BANANA PUDDING

Yield:
6 servings

Approx Per Serving:
Cal 777
Prot 15 g
Carbo 136 g
T Fat 22 g
25% Calories from Fat
Chol 210 mg
Fiber 2 g
Sod 373 mg

$^1/_4$ cup sugar
Salt to taste
1 (14-ounce) can sweetened condensed milk
$^1/_2$ cup milk
4 egg yolks, beaten
$^1/_2$ teaspoon vanilla extract
1 (16-ounce) package vanilla wafers
5 to 6 medium ripe bananas, sliced
4 egg whites
$^1/_4$ cup sugar

Combine $^1/_4$ cup sugar, salt, condensed milk and milk in double boiler; mix well. Stir in beaten egg yolks. Cook over boiling water until thickened, stirring constantly; reduce heat. Cook for 5 minutes, stirring occasionally. Remove from heat. Stir in vanilla. Layer vanilla wafers and bananas alternately in 2-quart ovenproof dish until all ingredients are used. Pour pudding over layers. Beat egg whites in mixer bowl until soft peaks form. Add $^1/_4$ cup sugar gradually, beating constantly until stiff peaks form. Spread over top. Bake at 425 degrees for 5 minutes or until light brown. Serve at room temperature or chill in refrigerator.

SOUR CREAM BANANA PUDDING

Yield:
8 servings

Approx Per Serving:
Cal 617
Prot 6 g
Carbo 93 g
T Fat 27 g
38% Calories from Fat
Chol 50 mg
Fiber 1 g
Sod 423 mg

1 (4-ounce) package vanilla instant pudding mix
1 cup milk
1/2 cup sugar
1 teaspoon vanilla extract
1 cup sour cream
12 ounces whipped topping
3 or 4 bananas, sliced
1 (16-ounce) package vanilla wafers

Combine pudding mix, milk and sugar in mixer bowl. Beat at medium speed until sugar dissolves. Add vanilla, sour cream and whipped topping. Beat at low speed until blended. Stir in bananas. Alternate layers of vanilla wafers and pudding mixture in bowl until all ingredients are used. Chill until serving time. May add drained crushed pineapple to pudding mixture.

OLD-FASHIONED BISCUIT PUDDING

Yield:
8 servings

Approx Per Serving:
Cal 342
Prot 7 g
Carbo 46 g
T Fat 15 g
39% Calories from Fat
Chol 102 mg
Fiber 1 g
Sod 312 mg

10 baked homemade biscuits, cut into halves
1/4 cup butter, softened
1/2 cup raisins
3/4 teaspoon cloves
3 eggs
3/4 cup sugar
1 tablespoon vanilla extract
1 1/2 cups milk

Spread cut sides of biscuits with butter. Layer in 6x9-inch baking dish. Sprinkle with raisins and cloves. Beat eggs and sugar in mixer bowl until blended. Add vanilla and milk; mix well. Pour over biscuits. May add additional milk to cover layers, but do not cover top layer of biscuits. Bake at 350 degrees until set and light brown.

BREAD PUDDING

Yield:
4 servings

Approx Per Serving:
Cal 323
Prot 11 g
Carbo 52 g
T Fat 8 g
22% Calories from Fat
Chol 124 mg
Fiber 1 g
Sod 306 mg

6 slices bread, torn into bite-sized pieces
2 eggs
2 cups milk
Salt to taste
1/2 cup sugar
1/4 teaspoon nutmeg
1/4 teaspoon cinnamon

Arrange bread in buttered baking dish. Beat eggs, milk, salt, sugar, nutmeg and cinnamon in mixer bowl until blended. Pour over bread. Bake at 350 degrees for 35 to 45 minutes or until set.

SAUCY BREAD PUDDING

Yield:
12 servings

Approx Per Serving:
Cal 438
Prot 6 g
Carbo 69 g
T Fat 16 g
31% Calories from Fat
Chol 104 mg
Fiber 2 g
Sod 285 mg

2 cups hot water
1 1/2 cups sugar
1 (12-ounce) can evaporated milk
4 eggs, beaten
1 cup flaked coconut
1/2 cup drained crushed pineapple
1/2 cup raisins
1/3 cup melted butter
1 teaspoon vanilla extract
1/2 teaspoon nutmeg
9 slices white bread, cut into 1/2-inch cubes
1 cup light corn syrup
1/4 cup butter
1/4 cup bourbon
1/2 teaspoon vanilla extract

Combine hot water and sugar in bowl, stirring until sugar dissolves. Whisk in evaporated milk and eggs until blended. Add coconut, pineapple, raisins, 1/3 cup melted butter, 1 teaspoon vanilla and nutmeg; mix well. Stir in bread cubes. Let stand for 30 minutes, stirring occasionally. Pour into greased 9x13-inch baking dish. Bake at 350 degrees for 45 minutes or until set. Bring corn syrup to a boil in saucepan. Cool slightly. Whisk in 1/4 cup butter, bourbon and 1/2 teaspoon vanilla until blended. Drizzle warm bourbon sauce over warm bread pudding.

FLAN

Yield:
8 servings

Approx Per Serving:
Cal 321
Prot 12 g
Carbo 44 g
T Fat 11 g
31% Calories from Fat
Chol 188 mg
Fiber 0 g
Sod 156 mg

¹/₂ cup sugar
6 eggs
1 (14-ounce) can sweetened condensed milk

1 (12-ounce) can evaporated milk
1 teaspoon vanilla extract

Sprinkle sugar in heavy skillet; do not stir. Cook over low heat until sugar melts and begins to form light brown syrup; stir to mix well. Pour into ovenproof mold, rotating to coat evenly. Cool slightly. Beat eggs slightly in bowl. Add condensed milk, evaporated milk and vanilla; mix well. Pour into prepared mold. Place in large pan with hot water to reach halfway up side of mold. Bake at 350 degrees for 25 minutes.

PUMPKIN PUDDING

Yield:
15 servings

Approx Per Serving:
Cal 262
Prot 4 g
Carbo 32 g
T Fat 14 g
47% Calories from Fat
Chol 49 mg
Fiber 1 g
Sod 328 mg

1 cup sugar
3 eggs, slightly beaten
1 (16-ounce) can pumpkin
1 (12-ounce) can evaporated milk
1 teaspoon cinnamon

¹/₂ teaspoon ginger
¹/₂ teaspoon salt
¹/₄ teaspoon ground cloves
¹/₂ (2-layer) package yellow cake mix
³/₄ cup melted margarine

Combine sugar, eggs, pumpkin, evaporated milk, cinnamon, ginger, salt and cloves in bowl; mix well. Spoon into greased 9x13-inch baking dish. Sprinkle with cake mix; drizzle with margarine. Bake at 350 degrees for 1 hour. Serve warm with whipped cream. May sprinkle with chopped nuts before baking.

PUNCH BOWL CAKE

Yield:
16 servings

Approx Per Serving:
Cal 542
Prot 7 g
Carbo 87 g
T Fat 20 g
32% Calories from Fat
Chol 42 mg
Fiber 3 g
Sod 619 mg

1 (2-layer) package yellow or white cake mix, baked, crumbled
2 (21-ounce) cans cherry pie filling
1 (20-ounce) can crushed pineapple, drained
2 (4-ounce) packages banana cream instant pudding mix, prepared
16 ounces whipped topping
1 (7-ounce) can flaked coconut

Layer 1/2 of the cake, 1/2 of the pie filling, 1/2 of the pineapple, 1/2 of the pudding, 1/4 of the whipped topping and 1/2 of the coconut in a punch bowl. Repeat layers. Spread top with remaining whipped topping. Chill until serving time.

EASY PUNCH BOWL CAKE

Yield:
16 servings

Approx Per Serving:
Cal 601
Prot 7 g
Carbo 95 g
T Fat 23 g
34% Calories from Fat
Chol 42 mg
Fiber 1 g
Sod 604 mg

1 (2-layer) package yellow cake mix, baked, crumbled
2 (6-ounce) packages vanilla instant pudding mix, prepared
2 (20-ounce) cans crushed pineapple, drained
2 (21-ounce) cans strawberry pie filling
32 ounces whipped topping
1 (4-ounce) jar maraschino cherries, drained

Layer cake, pudding, crushed pineapple, pie filling and whipped topping 1/2 at a time in order listed in large punch bowl. Sprinkle with maraschino cherries. Chill until serving time.

APPLE CAKE

Yield:
15 servings

*Approx Per
Serving:*
Cal 329
Prot 3 g
Carbo 51 g
T Fat 13 g
*35% Calories
from Fat*
Chol 42 mg
Fiber 1 g
Sod 137 mg

2 cups sugar
$2/3$ cup shortening
3 eggs
1 (16-ounce) can apples
2 cups flour
1 teaspoon baking
  powder
$1/2$ teaspoon baking soda
$1/2$ teaspoon ground
  cloves
$1/2$ teaspoon nutmeg
1 teaspoon allspice
1 teaspoon cinnamon
$1/2$ teaspoon salt
$1/2$ cup pecans
$1/2$ cup packed brown
  sugar

Cream sugar and shortening in mixer bowl until light and fluffy. Beat in eggs 1 at a time. Add undrained apples; mix well. Sift flour, baking powder, baking soda, cloves, nutmeg, allspice, cinnamon and salt together. Add to apple mixture; mix well. Spoon into greased and floured 9x13-inch cake pan. Sprinkle with pecans and brown sugar. Bake at 350 degrees for 35 to 45 minutes or until wooden pick inserted in center comes out clean. Cool on wire rack.

FRESH APPLE CAKE

Yield:
15 servings

*Approx Per
Serving:*
Cal 341
Prot 5 g
Carbo 55 g
T Fat 12 g
*32% Calories
from Fat*
Chol 57 mg
Fiber 2 g
Sod 161 mg

1 teaspoon baking soda
1 cup buttermilk
$1/2$ cup shortening
2 cups sugar
4 egg yolks
$2^{1}/_2$ cups flour
1 teaspoon cinnamon
1 teaspoon cloves
1 teaspoon nutmeg
1 teaspoon allspice
$1/2$ teaspoon salt
2 cups chopped apples
$2/3$ cup raisins
$2/3$ cup pecans
4 egg whites, stiffly
  beaten
$1/4$ cup confectioners'
  sugar

Mix baking soda with buttermilk in cup. Cream shortening and sugar in mixer bowl until light and fluffy. Beat in egg yolks. Add flour, cinnamon, cloves, nutmeg, allspice, salt and buttermilk; mix well. Stir in apples, raisins and pecans. Fold in beaten egg whites. Spoon into greased 9x13-inch cake pan. Bake at 350 degrees for 40 to 45 minutes or until cake tests done. Sprinkle with confectioners' sugar. Cool on wire rack.

APPLESAUCE CAKE

Yield:
15 servings

Approx Per Serving:
Cal 455
Prot 7 g
Carbo 78 g
T Fat 14 g
28% Calories from Fat
Chol 50 mg
Fiber 4 g
Sod 316 mg

1 cup walnuts or pecans
2 cups raisins
4 cups flour
3 tablespoons baking cocoa
²/₃ cup butter, softened
2 cups sugar
2 egg yolks
4 teaspoons baking soda
1 tablespoon cinnamon
2 tablespoons vanilla extract
3 cups unsweetened applesauce, cooked apples or dried fruit
2 egg whites, stiffly beaten

Toss walnuts and raisins with a small amount of the flour in bowl; set aside. Dissolve cocoa in a small amount of warm water in cup. Cream butter and sugar in mixer bowl until light and fluffy. Beat in egg yolks. Add remaining flour, baking soda, cocoa mixture, cinnamon and vanilla alternately with applesauce, mixing well after each addition. Fold in walnuts and raisins. Fold in egg whites. Spoon into greased and floured 9x13-inch cake pan. Bake at 325 degrees for 35 to 45 minutes or until wooden pick inserted in center comes out clean. Cool on wire rack.

CANDY BAR CAKE

Yield:
16 servings

Approx Per Serving:
Cal 496
Prot 6 g
Carbo 54 g
T Fat 30 g
53% Calories from Fat
Chol 62 mg
Fiber 1 g
Sod 337 mg

1 (2-layer) package golden butternut fudge cake mix
1¹/₂ cups milk
3 eggs
³/₄ cup vegetable oil
8 ounces cream cheese, softened
¹/₂ cup sugar
1 cup confectioners' sugar
12 ounces whipped topping
1 (8-ounce) chocolate candy bar, grated

Combine cake mix, milk, eggs and oil in mixer bowl; beat until smooth. Spoon into 3 greased and floured cake pans. Bake at 350 degrees for 20 to 30 minutes or until layers test done. Cool in pans for 10 minutes; remove to wire rack to cool completely. Combine cream cheese, sugar and confectioners' sugar in mixer bowl; beat until smooth. Fold in whipped topping and candy. Spread between layers and over top and side of cake.

BUTTERNUT CAKE

Yield:
16 servings

Approx Per
Serving:
Cal 565
Prot 5 g
Carbo 68 g
T Fat 32 g
49% Calories
from Fat
Chol 117 mg
Fiber 1 g
Sod 415 mg

1 cup butter, softened
2 cups sugar
1 teaspoon vanilla extract
$^1/_2$ teaspoon almond
  extract
1 tablespoon butternut
  extract
4 eggs
3 cups cake flour
2 teaspoons baking
  powder
$^1/_2$ teaspoon salt

1 cup minus 2
  tablespoons milk
$^1/_2$ cup butter or
  margarine, softened
8 ounces cream cheese,
  softened
1 (1-pound) package
  confectioners' sugar
2 teaspoons butternut
  extract
1 cup chopped pecans

Cream 1 cup butter in mixer bowl until light. Add sugar gradually, beating for 10 minutes. Add vanilla, almond extract and 1 tablespoon butternut extract. Beat in eggs 1 at a time. Sift flour, baking powder and salt together. Add to creamed mixture alternately with milk, mixing well after each addition. Spoon into greased and floured cake pans. Bake at 325 degrees for 15 to 20 minutes or until layers test done. Cool in pans for 10 minutes; remove to wire rack to cool completely. Cream $^1/_2$ cup butter, cream cheese and confectioners' sugar in mixer bowl until light and fluffy. Add 2 teaspoons butternut extract and chopped pecans; mix well. Spread between layers of cake.

Blueberry Cake

Cream $^1/_2$ cup butter with $^1/_2$ cup sugar and 2 eggs in bowl. Sift in $2^1/_2$ cups flour and 4 teaspoons baking powder alternately with $^1/_2$ cup milk. Toss $2^1/_2$ cups blueberries with enough flour to coat and fold into batter. Pour into a greased 9x13-inch cake pan and sprinkle with additional sugar. Bake at 400 degrees for 20 minutes, then at 375 degrees for 25 minutes.

CARROT AND PINEAPPLE CAKE

Yield:
15 servings

**Approx Per
Serving:**
Cal 479
Prot 4 g
Carbo 60 g
T Fat 26 g
48% Calories
from Fat
Chol 57 mg
Fiber 1 g
Sod 256 mg

1¹/2 cups flour
1 cup sugar
1 teaspoon baking
  powder
1 teaspoon baking soda
1 teaspoon cinnamon
¹/2 teaspoon salt
²/3 cup vegetable oil
2 eggs
1 cup finely shredded
  carrot
¹/2 cup crushed pineapple
1 teaspoon vanilla extract
6 ounces cream cheese,
  softened
¹/2 cup butter, softened
2 teaspoons vanilla
  extract
Salt to taste
5 cups sifted
  confectioners' sugar
1 cup chopped pecans

Mix flour, sugar, baking powder, baking soda, cinnamon and ¹/2 teaspoon salt in large bowl. Add oil, eggs, carrot, undrained pineapple and 1 teaspoon vanilla; mix until moistened. Beat at medium speed for 2 minutes. Spoon into greased and lightly floured 9x13-inch cake pan. Bake at 350 degrees for 25 to 30 minutes or until cake tests done. Cool on wire rack. Beat cream cheese and butter in mixer bowl until light and fluffy. Beat in 2 teaspoons vanilla and salt to taste. Add sifted confectioners' sugar gradually, beating until smooth. Mix in pecans. Spread over cake.

CHOCOLATE UPSIDE-DOWN CAKE

Yield:
15 servings

**Approx Per
Serving:**
Cal 517
Prot 4 g
Carbo 63 g
T Fat 29 g
49% Calories
from Fat
Chol 61 mg
Fiber 1 g
Sod 469 mg

1 cup shredded coconut
1 cup chopped pecans
1 (2-layer) package
  German chocolate
  cake mix
¹/2 cup margarine,
  softened
8 ounces cream cheese,
  softened
1 (1-pound) package
  confectioners' sugar

Mix coconut and pecans in bowl. Spread in greased 9x13-inch cake pan. Prepare cake mix using package directions. Spread in prepared pan. Heat margarine and cream cheese in saucepan just until softened. Add confectioners' sugar; mix well. Spread over cake batter. Bake at 350 degrees for 35 to 40 minutes or until cake tests done. Cool completely before serving.

FIVE-FLAVOR CAKE

Yield:
16 servings

Approx Per Serving:
Cal 475
Prot 5 g
Carbo 69 g
T Fat 20 g
38% Calories from Fat
Chol 68 mg
Fiber 1 g
Sod 183 mg

1 cup margarine, softened
1/2 cup shortening
3 cups sugar
5 eggs
3 cups flour
1 teaspoon baking powder
1 cup milk

1 teaspoon each coconut, butter, rum, lemon and vanilla extract
1 cup sugar
1/2 cup water
1 teaspoon each coconut, butter, rum, lemon and vanilla extract

Cream first 3 ingredients in mixer bowl until light and fluffy. Beat in eggs 1 at a time. Sift flour with baking powder. Add to creamed mixture alternately with milk, beating constantly. Add 1 teaspoon of each flavoring; mix well. Spoon into greased and floured 10-inch tube pan. Bake at 325 degrees for 1 1/2 hours. Cool in pan for 10 minutes. Combine 1 cup sugar, water and remaining flavorings in saucepan. Cook until sugar dissolves, stirring constantly. Spoon half the mixture over cake in pan. Let stand until glaze is absorbed; keep remaining glaze warm. Invert cake onto serving plate. Spoon remaining glaze over top. Do not use whipped margarine in this recipe.

LEMON FRUITCAKE

Yield:
20 servings

Approx Per Serving:
Cal 603
Prot 7 g
Carbo 65 g
T Fat 36 g
53% Calories from Fat
Chol 64 mg
Fiber 2 g
Sod 417 mg

2 cups margarine, softened
1 (1-pound) package brown sugar
6 egg yolks
2 cups self-rising flour
1 teaspoon baking powder

2 ounces lemon extract
8 ounces candied pineapple, chopped
8 ounces candied cherries
4 cups chopped pecans
2 cups flour
6 egg whites, stiffly beaten

Cream margarine and brown sugar in mixer bowl until light and fluffy. Beat in egg yolks. Add mixture of self-rising flour and baking powder; mix well. Mix in lemon extract. Toss pineapple, cherries and pecans with 2 cups flour in bowl. Fold into batter. Fold in eggs whites. Spoon into greased tube pan. Chill, covered, overnight. Bake at 250 degrees for 2 1/2 hours.

FRUITCAKE

Yield:
20 servings

*Approx Per
Serving:
Cal 407
Prot 4 g
Carbo 70 g
T Fat 14 g
30% Calories
from Fat
Chol 32 mg
Fiber 2 g
Sod 18 mg*

1/2 cup shortening
11/2 cups sugar
3 eggs
21/2 cups flour
1 teaspoon cinnamon
1 teaspoon cloves or
   allspice
1 teaspoon nutmeg
1/2 cup orange juice

1 cup strawberry
   preserves
8 ounces mixed candied
   fruit
8 ounces candied cherries
1 cup raisins
4 ounces dates, chopped
2 cups chopped pecans

Cream shortening and sugar in mixer bowl until light and fluffy. Beat in eggs. Mix flour, cinnamon, cloves and nutmeg together. Add to creamed mixture alternately with orange juice and preserves, mixing well after each addition. Fold in mixed fruit, cherries, raisins, dates and pecans. Spoon into greased and floured tube pan. Bake at 400 degrees for 10 minutes. Reduce oven temperature to 325 degrees. Bake for 1 hour and 50 minutes longer or until cake tests done. Cool in pan for 10 minutes; remove to wire rack to cool completely. May omit dates if preferred.

HOT MILK CAKE

Yield:
15 servings

*Approx Per
Serving:
Cal 249
Prot 4 g
Carbo 41 g
T Fat 8 g
29% Calories
from Fat
Chol 59 mg
Fiber <1 g
Sod 185 mg*

4 eggs
2 cups sugar
2 teaspoons vanilla
   extract
1/2 cup margarine

1 cup milk
2 cups flour
4 teaspoons baking
   powder

Combine eggs, sugar and vanilla in mixer bowl; beat until smooth. Melt margarine with milk in small saucepan. Add to egg mixture with flour and baking powder, mixing well; batter will be thin. Spoon into greased and floured 9x13-inch cake pan. Bake at 350 degrees until wooden pick inserted in center comes out clean. May add instant pudding if desired.

HUMMINGBIRD CAKE

Yield:
16 servings

Approx Per Serving:
Cal 723
Prot 6 g
Carbo 84 g
T Fat 43 g
52% Calories from Fat
Chol 55 mg
Fiber 2 g
Sod 307 mg

3 cups flour
2 cups sugar
1 teaspoon baking soda
1 teaspoon cinnamon
1 teaspoon salt
3 eggs, beaten
1 1/2 cups vegetable oil
1 1/2 teaspoons vanilla extract
1 (8-ounce) can crushed pineapple
2 cups mashed bananas
2 cups chopped pecans or walnuts
8 ounces cream cheese, softened
1/2 cup margarine, softened
1 (1-pound) package confectioners' sugar
1 teaspoon vanilla extract

Mix flour, sugar, baking soda, cinnamon and salt in large bowl. Add eggs and oil; mix by hand until moistened. Stir in 1 1/2 teaspoons vanilla, pineapple, bananas and pecans. Spoon into greased and floured bundt pan. Bake at 350 degrees for 30 to 35 minutes or until cake tests done. Cool in pan for 10 minutes; remove to wire rack to cool completely. Combine cream cheese and margarine in mixer bowl; beat until smooth. Add confectioners' sugar; beat until fluffy. Add 1 teaspoon vanilla; mix well. Spread over cake. May bake in 9x13-inch cake pan or three 9-inch cake pans if preferred.

LEMON CAKE

Yield:
16 servings

Approx Per Serving:
Cal 486
Prot 5 g
Carbo 54 g
T Fat 29 g
52% Calories from Fat
Chol 144 mg
Fiber <1 g
Sod 442 mg

2 cups butter, softened
3 cups sugar
6 eggs
4 cups cake flour
1 teaspoon baking powder
1/2 teaspoon salt
1 cup milk
2 teaspoons lemon extract
1 teaspoon vanilla extract

Cream butter and sugar in mixer bowl until light and fluffy. Beat in eggs 1 at a time. Sift flour with baking powder and salt. Add to creamed mixture alternately with milk. Add flavorings; mix well. Spoon into greased and floured tube pan. Bake at 325 degrees for 1 1/2 hours or until cake tests done. Cool in pan for 10 minutes; remove to wire rack to cool completely.

LEMON PUDDING CAKE

Yield:
6 servings

Approx Per Serving:
Cal 273
Prot 6 g
Carbo 40 g
T Fat 11 g
34% Calories from Fat
Chol 162 mg
Fiber <1 g
Sod 209 mg

3 tablespoons butter, softened
1 cup sugar
4 egg yolks
3 tablespoons flour
1/4 teaspoon salt
1/3 cup lemon juice
2 teaspoons grated lemon rind
1 cup milk
4 egg whites, stiffly beaten

Cream butter in mixer bowl until light. Add sugar gradually, beating until fluffy. Beat in egg yolks. Stir in flour, salt, lemon juice and lemon rind. Add milk gradually, mixing well. Fold in egg whites. Spoon into shallow 1 1/2-quart baking dish; place in 9x13-inch pan of hot water. Bake at 325 degrees for 40 minutes. Increase oven temperature to 350 degrees. Bake for 10 minutes longer. Serve warm or cooled, plain or with whipped cream.

ITALIAN CREAM CAKE

Yield:
16 servings

Approx Per Serving:
Cal 575
Prot 6 g
Carbo 70 g
T Fat 32 g
48% Calories from Fat
Chol 113 mg
Fiber 2 g
Sod 248 mg

1 teaspoon baking soda
1 cup buttermilk
1/2 cup butter, softened
1/2 cup shortening
2 cups sugar
5 egg yolks
2 cups flour
1 teaspoon vanilla extract
5 egg whites, stiffly beaten
1 cup chopped pecans
1 (3-ounce) can coconut
8 ounces cream cheese, softened
1/2 cup butter, softened
1 (1-pound) package confectioners' sugar
1 teaspoon vanilla extract

Dissolve baking soda in buttermilk in cup; let stand for several minutes. Cream 1/2 cup butter, shortening and sugar in mixer bowl until fluffy. Beat in egg yolks 1 at a time. Add flour alternately with buttermilk mixture, mixing well after each addition. Stir in 1 teaspoon vanilla. Fold in egg whites, pecans and coconut. Spoon into 3 greased and floured cake pans. Bake at 325 degrees for 25 to 30 minutes or until layers test done. Cool in pans for 5 minutes; remove to wire rack to cool completely. Combine cream cheese and 1/2 cup butter in mixer bowl; beat until smooth. Add remaining ingredients; mix well. Spread between layers and over top and side of cake.

ORANGE CAKE

Yield:
15 servings

Approx Per Serving:
Cal 307
Prot 4 g
Carbo 59 g
T Fat 7 g
21% Calories from Fat
Chol 45 mg
Fiber 2 g
Sod 146 mg

1 teaspoon baking soda
1 cup buttermilk
1 cup ground raisins
2 orange rinds, ground
1/2 cup butter, softened

1 cup sugar
2 eggs
2 cups flour
1 cup sugar
Juice of 2 oranges

Dissolve baking soda in buttermilk in cup; set aside. Mix raisins and orange rinds in small bowl. Cream butter and 1 cup sugar in mixer bowl until light and fluffy. Beat in eggs. Add flour alternately with buttermilk mixture, mixing well after each addition. Stir in raisin mixture. Spoon into greased and floured 9x13-inch cake pan. Bake at 325 degrees until wooden pick inserted in center comes out clean. Heat 1 cup sugar with orange juice in saucepan until sugar dissolves. Spoon glaze over hot cake. Cool on wire rack.

PEANUT BUTTER CAKE

Yield:
16 servings

Approx Per Serving:
Cal 458
Prot 8 g
Carbo 67 g
T Fat 19 g
36% Calories from Fat
Chol 61 mg
Fiber <1 g
Sod 379 mg

2 cups flour
1 teaspoon baking powder
1 teaspoon baking soda
1 teaspoon salt
1/2 cup butter, softened
1 1/4 cups sugar
9 ounces peanut butter chips, melted
2 eggs

1 teaspoon vanilla extract
1 1/2 cups milk
3 ounces peanut butter chips, melted
8 ounces cream cheese, softened
1 teaspoon vanilla extract
1 (1-pound) package confectioners' sugar
2 tablespoons milk

Sift first 4 ingredients together. Cream butter and sugar in mixer bowl until light and fluffy. Blend in 9 ounces melted peanut butter chips. Beat in eggs and vanilla. Add flour mixture alternately with 1 1/2 cups milk, mixing well after each addition. Spoon evenly into greased and floured 9-inch cake pans. Bake at 350 degrees for 35 to 40 minutes or until wooden pick inserted in center comes out clean. Cool on wire rack. Blend remaining 3 ounces melted peanut butter chips with cream cheese and vanilla in mixer bowl. Add remaining ingredients; mix well. Spread between layers and over top and side of cake.

PIG CAKE

Yield:
15 servings

**Approx Per
Serving:**
Cal 404
Prot 4 g
Carbo 65 g
T Fat 15 g
33% Calories
from Fat
Chol 57 mg
Fiber 1 g
Sod 428 mg

1 (2-layer) package
  yellow cake mix
1/2 cup orange juice
1/2 cup margarine,
  softened
4 eggs
2 (11-ounce) cans
  mandarin oranges,
  drained

1 (4-ounce) package
  vanilla instant
  pudding mix
1 (11-ounce) can
  crushed pineapple
2 cups confectioners'
  sugar
8 ounces whipped
  topping

Beat first 3 ingredients in mixer bowl at medium speed until smooth. Add eggs 1 at a time, mixing for 1 minute after each addition. Add oranges; mix just until oranges are slightly chopped. Spoon into greased and floured 9x13-inch cake pan. Bake at 350 degrees for 25 minutes or until brown. Mix pudding mix and pineapple in mixer bowl. Beat in confectioners' sugar gradually. Fold in whipped topping. Spread over cake. Store in refrigerator.

PINA COLADA CAKE

Yield:
15 servings

**Approx Per
Serving:**
Cal 731
Prot 8 g
Carbo 80 g
T Fat 44 g
53% Calories
from Fat
Chol 117 mg
Fiber 3 g
Sod 364 mg

1 (2-layer) package
  butter-recipe golden
  cake mix
1/2 cup margarine,
  softened
3 eggs
1 cup water
1 (12-ounce) can cream
  of coconut
1 (14-ounce) can
  sweetened condensed
  milk

1 (16-ounce) can
  crushed pineapple,
  drained
2 cups confectioners'
  sugar, sifted
12 ounces whipped
  topping
2 cups sour cream
1 (12-ounce) package
  frozen coconut, thawed

Beat cake mix, margarine, eggs and water in mixer bowl until smooth. Spoon into 9x13-inch cake pan. Bake using cake mix directions. Pierce holes in hot cake. Drizzle with mixture of cream of coconut and condensed milk. Cool. Spread with pineapple. Spread mixture of confectioners' sugar, whipped topping and sour cream over pineapple. Top with coconut. Store in refrigerator.

PINEAPPLE CAKE

Yield:
16 servings

Approx Per
Serving:
Cal 440
Prot 4 g
Carbo 63 g
T Fat 20 g
40% Calories
from Fat
Chol 55 mg
Fiber 1 g
Sod 249 mg

2 (20-ounce) cans
crushed pineapple
1 cup shortening
1 1/2 cups sugar
3 eggs
1 tablespoon vanilla
extract
3 cups sifted flour

3 3/4 teaspoons baking
powder
3/4 teaspoon salt
1/2 cup butter
1 cup (about) sugar
2 tablespoons cornstarch
1/2 cup (or more) water

Drain pineapple, reserving juice. Add enough water to reserved juice to measure 1 cup. Cream shortening and 1 1/2 cups sugar in mixer bowl until light and fluffy. Beat in eggs and vanilla. Sift in flour, baking powder and salt; mix well. Spoon into 3 cake pans sprayed with baking spray. Bake at 350 degrees for 35 to 40 minutes or just until layers begin to pull from sides of pans. Cool in pans for 10 minutes; remove to wire rack to cool completely. Combine pineapple, butter and 1 cup sugar in medium saucepan. Blend cornstarch with 1/2 cup water in cup. Stir into saucepan. Cook until thickened, stirring constantly. Spread hot frosting between layers and over top and side of cake.

BROWN SUGAR POUND CAKE

Yield:
16 servings

Approx Per
Serving:
Cal 510
Prot 4 g
Carbo 66 g
T Fat 26 g
45% Calories
from Fat
Chol 113 mg
Fiber 1 g
Sod 274 mg

1 1/2 cups butter, softened
2 cups sugar
1 (1-pound) package
light brown sugar
3 cups cake flour

5 eggs
1/4 cup dark rum
1 teaspoon vanilla extract
1 cup pecans

Cream butter, sugar and brown sugar in mixer bowl until light and fluffy. Add flour alternately with eggs, mixing well for 2 to 3 minutes. Add rum, vanilla and pecans; mix well. Spoon into greased and floured tube pan. Bake at 325 degrees for 1 3/4 to 2 hours or until cake tests done. Cool in pan for 10 minutes; invert onto wire rack to cool completely.

BUTTERMILK POUND CAKE

Yield:
16 servings

Approx Per
Serving:
Cal 378
Prot 5 g
Carbo 56 g
T Fat 15 g
36% Calories
from Fat
Chol 80 mg
Fiber 1 g
Sod 120 mg

1 cup shortening
3 cups sugar
6 eggs, at room
  temperature
1¹/₂ teaspoons vanilla
  extract

3 cups flour
¹/₄ teaspoon baking soda
¹/₂ teaspoon salt
1 cup buttermilk

Cream shortening and sugar in mixer bowl until light and fluffy. Beat in eggs 1 at a time. Add vanilla; mix well. Mix flour, baking soda and salt together. Add to creamed mixture alternately with buttermilk, mixing well after each addition. Spoon into greased and floured 10-inch tube pan. Bake at 325 degrees for 1¹/₄ hours. Cool in pan for 10 minutes; remove to wire rack to cool completely. May use butter-flavored shortening if desired.

CREAM CHEESE POUND CAKE

Yield:
16 servings

Approx Per
Serving:
Cal 457
Prot 5 g
Carbo 50 g
T Fat 27 g
53% Calories
from Fat
Chol 96 mg
Fiber <1 g
Sod 267 mg

¹/₂ cup shortening
1 cup margarine or
  butter, softened
3 cups sugar
8 ounces cream cheese,
  softened

3 cups cake flour
6 eggs
1 tablespoon vanilla
  extract

Cream shortening and margarine in mixer bowl until light. Add sugar 1 cup at a time, beating until fluffy. Add cream cheese gradually, beating constantly. Add flour alternately with eggs, mixing well after each addition. Beat in vanilla. Spoon into tube pan sprayed with baking spray. Bake at 325 degrees for 1¹/₄ hours. Cool in pan for 10 minutes; remove to wire rack to cool completely.

LEMON AND APRICOT POUND CAKE

Yield:
16 servings

Approx Per Serving:
Cal 272
Prot 3 g
Carbo 42 g
T Fat 11 g
35% Calories from Fat
Chol 53 mg
Fiber <1 g
Sod 219 mg

1 (2-layer) package lemon cake mix
4 eggs
1/2 cup sugar
1/2 cup vegetable oil
1 cup apricot nectar
1 cup sifted confectioners' sugar
5 tablespoons lemon juice

Combine cake mix, eggs, sugar, oil and apricot nectar in mixer bowl; beat until smooth. Spoon into greased and floured bundt pan. Bake at 350 degrees for 1 hour. Cool in pan for 10 minutes; remove to serving plate. Drizzle mixture of confectioners' sugar and lemon juice over cake. Let stand until cool.

MOM'S POUND CAKE

Yield:
16 servings

Approx Per Serving:
Cal 436
Prot 5 g
Carbo 59 g
T Fat 20 g
41% Calories from Fat
Chol 99 mg
Fiber 1 g
Sod 145 mg

1 cup butter, softened
1/2 cup vegetable oil or shortening
3 cups sugar
5 eggs
1 cup milk
1 teaspoon vanilla extract
1 teaspoon almond extract
3 1/2 cups flour, sifted

Combine butter, oil and sugar in mixer bowl; beat until light. Beat in eggs 1 at a time. Mix milk and flavorings. Add to beaten mixture alternately with flour, beginning and ending with flour and mixing well after each addition. Spoon into large tube pan sprayed with baking spray. Bake at 325 degrees for 1 hour and 35 minutes. Cool in pan for 10 minutes; remove to wire rack to cool completely. May substitute lemon extract for almond extract or 8 ounces cream cheese for 1/2 cup of the butter.

OLD-FASHIONED POUND CAKE

Yield:
16 servings

Approx Per Serving:
Cal 426
Prot 5 g
Carbo 57 g
T Fat 20 g
42% Calories from Fat
Chol 128 mg
Fiber 1 g
Sod 263 mg

1¹/₂ cups butter or margarine, softened
3 cups sugar
1 tablespoon vanilla extract
1 teaspoon lemon extract
1 tablespoon fresh lemon juice

1 teaspoon grated lemon rind
6 eggs
3 cups flour
1 teaspoon baking powder
¹/₄ teaspoon salt
¹/₂ cup evaporated milk

Cream butter in large mixer bowl until light. Add sugar ¹/₂ cup at a time, mixing well after each addition. Stir in flavorings, lemon juice and lemon rind. Beat in eggs 1 at a time. Sift flour, baking powder and salt together. Add to creamed mixture alternately with evaporated milk, mixing well after each addition. Spoon into greased and floured 10-inch tube pan. Bake at 325 degrees for 1 hour and 10 minutes to 1 hour and 20 minutes or until wooden pick inserted in center comes out clean. Cool in pan for 20 minutes; remove to wire rack to cool completely.

SOUR CREAM POUND CAKE

Yield:
16 servings

Approx Per Serving:
Cal 384
Prot 5 g
Carbo 55 g
T Fat 17 g
38% Calories from Fat
Chol 117 mg
Fiber 1 g
Sod 162 mg

1 cup butter, softened
3 cups sugar
6 eggs
1 cup sour cream

¹/₄ teaspoon baking soda
1 teaspoon vanilla extract
3 cups sifted flour

Grease and flour 10-inch tube pan; line bottom with waxed paper. Cream butter in mixer bowl until light. Add sugar gradually, beating until fluffy. Beat in eggs 1 at a time. Beat in mixture of sour cream and baking soda. Add vanilla; mix well. Fold in sifted flour gradually. Spoon into prepared tube pan. Bake at 350 degrees for 1¹/₂ hours or until cake tests done. Cool in pan for 10 minutes. Invert onto wire rack and remove waxed paper; let stand until cool.

GLAZED SOUR CREAM POUND CAKE

Yield:
16 servings

Approx Per Serving:
Cal 460
Prot 4 g
Carbo 57 g
T Fat 25 g
48% Calories
from Fat
Chol 104 mg
Fiber <1 g
Sod 299 mg

3 cups cake flour
1 teaspoon baking powder
1/2 teaspoon salt
1 cup butter, softened
1/2 cup shortening
3 cups sugar

5 eggs
1 cup sour cream
1 teaspoon vanilla extract
1 teaspoon lemon extract
Juice of 1/2 lemon
1 cup confectioners' sugar

Sift flour, baking powder and salt together 3 times; set aside. Cream butter and shortening in mixer bowl until light. Add sugar; beat until fluffy. Beat in eggs 1 at a time. Add flour mixture alternately with sour cream, mixing well after each addition. Beat in flavorings. Spoon into greased and floured tube pan. Bake at 350 degrees for 1 to 1 1/4 hours or until cake tests done. Cool in pan for 10 minutes. Remove to serving plate. Drizzle with mixture of lemon juice and confectioners' sugar.

ORANGE CRUSH POUND CAKE

Yield:
16 servings

Approx Per Serving:
Cal 524
Prot 5 g
Carbo 70 g
T Fat 26 g
43% Calories
from Fat
Chol 97 mg
Fiber 1 g
Sod 127 mg

1 cup shortening
1/4 cup butter, softened
2 3/4 cups sugar
5 eggs
3 cups flour
1 cup Orange Crush soda
1 teaspoon orange extract
1 teaspoon vanilla extract

6 ounces cream cheese, softened
6 tablespoons butter, softened
2 cups confectioners' sugar
1 teaspoon orange extract
1/2 teaspoon vanilla extract

Cream shortening, 1/4 cup butter and sugar in mixer bowl for 10 minutes. Beat in eggs 1 at a time. Add flour alternately with orange soda, mixing well after each addition. Beat in 1 teaspoon orange extract and 1 teaspoon vanilla. Spoon into greased and floured 10-inch tube pan. Bake at 350 degrees for 1 hour and 10 minutes or until wooden pick inserted near center comes out clean. Cool in pan for 15 minutes; remove to serving plate to cool completely. Combine remaining ingredients in mixer bowl; beat until smooth. Spread on cooled cake.

EASY PUMPKIN CAKE

Yield:
16 servings

Approx Per Serving:
Cal 263
Prot 3 g
Carbo 37 g
T Fat 12 g
40% Calories from Fat
Chol 54 mg
Fiber 1 g
Sod 227 mg

1 (2-layer) package
    yellow cake mix
³/4 cup sugar
¹/2 cup vegetable oil
¹/2 cup water

1 (16-ounce) can
    pumpkin
4 eggs
1 teaspoon cinnamon
¹/8 teaspoon nutmeg

Combine cake mix, sugar, oil, water, pumpkin, eggs, cinnamon and nutmeg in mixer bowl; beat until smooth. Spoon into greased and floured bundt pan. Bake at 350 degrees for 1 hour. Cool in pan for 10 minutes; remove to wire rack to cool completely. May dust with confectioners' sugar if desired.

RED VELVET CAKE

Yield:
16 servings

Approx Per Serving:
Cal 595
Prot 5 g
Carbo 63 g
T Fat 37 g
55% Calories from Fat
Chol 43 mg
Fiber 1 g
Sod 190 mg

2¹/2 cups sifted flour
1¹/2 cups sugar
¹/4 teaspoon baking
    powder
1 teaspoon baking soda
1 teaspoon baking cocoa
1 cup buttermilk
1¹/2 cups vegetable oil
1 teaspoon vinegar
2 eggs
1 (1-ounce) bottle of red
    food coloring

1 teaspoon vanilla extract
1 teaspoon butternut
    extract
¹/2 cup margarine,
    softened
8 ounces cream cheese,
    softened
1 (1-pound) package
    confectioners' sugar
¹/2 teaspoon vanilla
    extract
1 cup chopped pecans

Sift first 5 ingredients into bowl. Add buttermilk, oil, vinegar, eggs, food coloring, 1 teaspoon vanilla and butternut extract in order listed, mixing well. Spoon into 3 greased and floured cake pans. Bake at 350 degrees for 25 minutes or until layers test done. Cool in pans for 10 minutes; remove to wire rack to cool completely. Combine margarine and cream cheese in mixer bowl; beat until light. Add remaining ingredients; mix well. Spread between layers and over top and side of cake.

PEACHY STRAWBERRY CAKE

Yield:
16 servings

**Approx Per
Serving:**
Cal 277
Prot 3 g
Carbo 40 g
T Fat 12 g
39% Calories
from Fat
Chol 30 mg
Fiber 1 g
Sod 254 mg

1 (2-layer) package
  yellow cake mix
16 ounces whipped
  topping

1 teaspoon vanilla extract
1 (16-ounce) can sliced
  peaches, drained
2 cups sliced strawberries

Prepare and bake cake using package directions for 2 layers. Cool in pans for 10 minutes; remove to wire rack to cool completely. Mix whipped topping with vanilla in bowl. Spread 1/4 of the whipped topping on 1 cake layer. Arrange peaches and sliced strawberries on prepared layer. Top with remaining layer. Spread remaining whipped topping over top and side of cake. Garnish with whole strawberries.

STRAWBERRY SHORTCAKE

Yield:
15 servings

**Approx Per
Serving:**
Cal 232
Prot 3 g
Carbo 37 g
T Fat 8 g
31% Calories
from Fat
Chol 0 mg
Fiber 2 g
Sod 287 mg

1 (2-layer) package
  white cake mix
1 small package
  sugar-free strawberry
  gelatin

8 ounces whipped
  topping
15 to 20 strawberries

Prepare and bake cake using package directions for 9x13-inch cake pan. Punch holes in warm cake with handle of wooden spoon. Prepare gelatin using package directions. Drizzle into holes and over top of cake. Spread with whipped topping; top with strawberries. Chill until serving time.

BLACKBERRY PIE

Yield:
6 servings

Approx Per
Serving:
Cal 432
Prot 4 g
Carbo 62 g
T Fat 20 g
40% Calories
from Fat
Chol 5 mg
Fiber 6 g
Sod 198 mg

2/3 cup sugar
3 tablespoons cornstarch
3 to 4 cups blackberries
1 1/2 cups sifted flour
1/2 teaspoon salt
1/2 cup shortening

4 to 5 tablespoons water
Salt to taste
1 tablespoon melted
  butter
1 tablespoon sugar

Combine 2/3 cup sugar and cornstarch in bowl. Add blackberries; mix well. Sift flour and 1/2 teaspoon salt in bowl. Cut in shortening until crumbly. Sprinkle with water, mixing with fork just until moistened. Shape dough into 2 balls. Flatten each ball slightly on lightly floured surface. Roll to fit pie plate from center to edge of pastry. Roll 1 pastry portion over rolling pin; unroll over pie plate. Fit loosely onto bottom and side of pie plate. Spoon blackberry mixture into pastry-lined pie shell. Sprinkle with salt to taste; drizzle with butter. Moisten edges with water. Top with remaining pastry. Trim 1 inch beyond edge; tuck under edge of bottom pastry. Crimp edges. Prick top with fork or cut vents. Sprinkle with 1 tablespoon sugar. Bake at 400 degrees for 40 to 50 minutes or until light brown. May substitute elderberries or raspberries for blackberries.

Mock Apple Pie

Sauté 2 sliced apples in 2 tablespoons reduced-calorie margarine for 2 minutes in large nonstick skillet. Add 1/4 cup thawed frozen apple juice concentrate, 1 tablespoon brown sugar, 1/2 teaspoon lemon juice, 1/2 teaspoon cinnamon and 1/4 teaspoon nutmeg. Cook until liquid is syrupy. Add 3 ounces bowtie pasta that has been cooked and drained and toss gently. Serve warm with a sprinkle of confectioners' sugar or a scoop of ice milk or frozen yogurt sprinkled with cinnamon.

BUTTERMILK AND LEMON PIES

Yield:
12 servings

*Approx Per
Serving:
Cal 451
Prot 10 g
Carbo 62 g
T Fat 19 g
37% Calories
from Fat
Chol 140 mg
Fiber 1 g
Sod 347 mg*

2 cups sugar
1/4 cup plus 3
  tablespoons cornstarch
5 cups buttermilk
3 ounces cream cheese,
  softened
7 egg yolks
2 teaspoons grated
  lemon rind
1/4 cup lemon juice
2 tablespoons butter
1 teaspoon lemon extract
2 baked (9-inch) pie
  shells
7 egg whites
3/4 teaspoon cream of
  tartar
1/4 cup plus 3
  tablespoons
  confectioners' sugar
1/4 teaspoon lemon
  extract

Combine sugar and cornstarch in heavy saucepan; mix well. Add buttermilk gradually, stirring until blended. Add cream cheese. Cook over medium heat until mixture thickens and comes to a boil, stirring constantly. Boil for 1 minute, stirring occasionally. Beat egg yolks in mixer bowl until thick and lemon-colored. Stir about 1/4 of the hot cream cheese mixture into egg yolks; stir egg yolks into hot mixture. Cook for 2 to 3 minutes or until blended, stirring constantly. Remove from heat. Stir in lemon rind, lemon juice, butter and 1 teaspoon lemon extract. Spoon into pie shells. Beat egg whites and cream of tartar in mixer bowl for 1 minute. Add confectioners' sugar 1 tablespoon at a time, beating constantly until stiff peaks form. Beat in 1/4 teaspoon lemon extract. Spread over hot filling, sealing to edge. Bake at 350 degrees for 12 to 15 minutes or until light brown.

Hello Dolly Pie

Pour a mixture of 1 cup each coconut, chocolate chips and pecans and a 14-ounce can of sweetened condensed milk into a graham cracker pie shell. Bake at 350 degrees for 30 minutes. Serve in very small slices.

SOUTHERN LEMON CHESS PIE

Yield:
6 servings

**Approx Per
Serving:**
*Cal 459
Prot 6 g
Carbo 68 g
T Fat 19 g
37% Calories
from Fat
Chol 123 mg
Fiber 1 g
Sod 258 mg*

3 eggs
1¹/₂ cups sugar
1 tablespoon flour
1 tablespoon cornmeal
¹/₄ cup milk
3 tablespoons melted
 butter

¹/₄ cup lemon juice
1 teaspoon lemon extract
1 unbaked (9-inch) pie
 shell

Beat eggs in mixer bowl until frothy. Add sugar gradually, beating until mixture is lemon-colored. Beat in flour and cornmeal until blended. Add milk, butter, lemon juice and lemon extract; mix well. Spoon into pie shell. Bake at 375 degrees for 45 to 55 minutes or until set.

CHOCOLATE CHESS PIE

Yield:
8 servings

**Approx Per
Serving:**
*Cal 493
Prot 5 g
Carbo 68 g
T Fat 24 g
42% Calories
from Fat
Chol 59 mg
Fiber 1 g
Sod 339 mg*

1¹/₂ cups sugar
3 tablespoons (heaping)
 baking cocoa
2 eggs, beaten
¹/₂ cup melted margarine
1 teaspoon vanilla extract
1 (5-ounce) can
 evaporated milk

1 unbaked (10-inch)
 deep-dish pie shell
1 cup confectioners'
 sugar
1 teaspoon baking cocoa
2 to 3 tablespoons (or
 more) milk

Sift sugar and 3 tablespoons cocoa into bowl. Stir in eggs, margarine, vanilla and evaporated milk. Pour into pie shell. Bake at 350 degrees for 55 to 60 minutes or until set. Remove to wire rack to cool. Combine confectioners sugar and 1 teaspoon cocoa in bowl; mix well. Stir in milk until of glaze consistency. Drizzle over cooled pie.

CHOCOLATE FUDGE PIE

Yield:
6 servings

Approx Per Serving:
Cal 441
Prot 5 g
Carbo 54 g
T Fat 24 g
48% Calories from Fat
Chol 71 mg
Fiber 2 g
Sod 319 mg

1 cup sugar
1/4 cup flour
1/4 cup baking cocoa
6 tablespoons melted margarine, cooled
2 eggs, beaten
1 teaspoon vanilla extract
1 unbaked (9-inch) pie shell

Combine sugar, flour and cocoa in bowl; mix well. Stir in margarine and eggs. Add vanilla; mix well. Spoon into pie shell. Place on bottom rack of oven. Bake at 325 degrees for 30 minutes. Remove to wire rack to cool.

CHOCOLATE PIE

Yield:
6 servings

Approx Per Serving:
Cal 530
Prot 9 g
Carbo 68 g
T Fat 26 g
44% Calories from Fat
Chol 117 mg
Fiber 2 g
Sod 443 mg

1 cup sugar
1 tablespoon (heaping) flour
1/4 teaspoon salt
1/3 cup baking cocoa
2 cups milk
3 egg yolks, beaten
1/3 cup margarine
1 teaspoon vanilla extract
1 baked (9-inch) pie shell
3 egg whites
6 tablespoons sugar

Combine 1 cup sugar, flour, salt and cocoa in saucepan; mix well. Stir in milk and egg yolks. Cook until thickened, stirring constantly. Remove from heat; stir in margarine and vanilla. Spoon into pie shell. Beat egg whites in mixer bowl until soft peaks form. Add 6 tablespoons sugar gradually, beating constantly until stiff peaks form. Spread over hot filling, sealing to edge. Bake at 350 degrees until light brown.

OLD-FASHIONED CHOCOLATE PIE

Yield:
6 servings

*Approx Per
Serving:*
Cal 493
Prot 10 g
Carbo 70 g
T Fat 21 g
*37% Calories
from Fat*
Chol 152 mg
Fiber 2 g
Sod 334 mg

4 egg yolks
1 cup sugar
1/4 cup baking cocoa
3 tablespoons cornstarch
2 cups milk
1/2 teaspoon vanilla
   extract
1/8 teaspoon salt

2 tablespoons margarine
1 baked (9-inch) pie shell
4 egg whites, at room
   temperature
6 tablespoons sugar
1/2 teaspoon vanilla
   extract

Beat egg yolks and 1 cup sugar in bowl until lemon-colored. Stir in mixture of cocoa and cornstarch. Add milk, 1/2 teaspoon vanilla and salt; mix well. Pour into double boiler. Cook over simmering water until thickened, stirring constantly. Stir in margarine. Spoon into baked pie shell. Beat egg whites in mixer bowl at medium speed until frothy. Add 6 tablespoons sugar 1 tablespoon at a time, beating constantly. Add 1/2 teaspoon vanilla; mix well. Beat at high speed until stiff and glossy. Spread over hot filling, sealing to edge. Bake at 300 degrees for 20 minutes.

CHOCOLATE CHIP PIE

Yield:
8 servings

*Approx Per
Serving:*
Cal 658
Prot 7 g
Carbo 57 g
T Fat 48 g
*63% Calories
from Fat*
Chol 115 mg
Fiber 3 g
Sod 381 mg

2 eggs
1/2 cup flour
1/2 cup sugar
1/2 cup packed brown
   sugar
1 cup melted butter,
   cooled

1 cup semisweet
   chocolate chips
1 cup chopped walnuts
1 unbaked (9-inch) pie
   shell

Beat eggs in mixer bowl until frothy. Add flour, sugar and brown sugar, beating until blended. Add butter; mix well. Stir in chocolate chips and walnuts. Spoon into pie shell. Bake at 325 degrees for 1 hour.

COCONUT PIES

Yield:
12 servings

Approx Per
Serving:
Cal 366
Prot 6 g
Carbo 35 g
T Fat 23 g
55% Calories
from Fat
Chol 87 mg
Fiber 3 g
Sod 312 mg

4 eggs, beaten
1/2 cup sugar
1/2 cup self-rising flour
2 cups milk
1 teaspoon vanilla extract
1/4 cup butter, softened
1 (7-ounce) can coconut
2 unbaked (9-inch) pie
   shells

Combine eggs, sugar and flour in bowl; mix well. Stir in milk, vanilla, butter and coconut. Pour into pie shells. Bake at 350 degrees for 30 to 40 minutes or until set. May bake in 10-inch deep-dish pie shell.

QUICK AND EASY COCONUT PIE

Yield:
6 servings

Approx Per
Serving:
Cal 491
Prot 6 g
Carbo 54 g
T Fat 29 g
52% Calories
from Fat
Chol 138 mg
Fiber 2 g
Sod 336 mg

6 tablespoons melted
   butter, cooled
3 eggs, beaten
1 cup sugar
1/2 cup buttermilk
1 cup flaked coconut
1 unbaked (9-inch) pie
   shell

Combine butter, eggs, sugar, buttermilk and coconut in bowl; mix well. Spoon into pie shell. Bake at 350 degrees for 30 to 40 minutes or until set.

Buett Residence   871 Oakdale Atlanta, Georgia

ORANGE PIE

Yield:
6 servings

Approx Per Serving:
Cal 468
Prot 6 g
Carbo 75 g
T Fat 17 g
32% Calories from Fat
Chol 116 mg
Fiber 1 g
Sod 234 mg

1 cup sugar
5 tablespoons cornstarch
1 cup orange juice
1 cup orange sections, chopped
2 tablespoons grated orange rind
3 egg yolks, beaten
2 tablespoons lemon juice
2 tablespoons butter
1 baked (9-inch) pie shell, cooled
3 egg whites
6 tablespoons sugar
1/2 teaspoon vanilla extract

Combine 1 cup sugar and cornstarch in saucepan; mix well. Stir in orange juice, orange sections and orange rind. Cook over low heat until thickened, stirring constantly. Stir a small amount of hot mixture into egg yolks; stir egg yolks into hot mixture. Cook for 5 minutes, stirring frequently. Remove from heat. Stir in lemon juice and butter. Cool. Pour into pie shell. Beat egg whites in mixer bowl until soft peaks form. Add 6 tablespoons sugar gradually, beating constantly until stiff peaks form. Beat in vanilla. Spread over filling, sealing to edge. Bake at 350 degrees until light brown.

PEANUT BUTTER PIE

Yield:
8 servings

Approx Per Serving:
Cal 762
Prot 17 g
Carbo 59 g
T Fat 55 g
62% Calories from Fat
Chol 89 mg
Fiber 4 g
Sod 565 mg

1 1/2 cups graham cracker crumbs
1/2 cup melted butter
2 quarts vanilla ice cream, softened
1 (12-ounce) jar (or less) crunchy peanut butter
1/2 cup chopped pecans

Combine graham cracker crumbs and butter in bowl; mix well. Pat evenly over bottom and side of 10-inch pie plate. Freeze until firm. Combine ice cream and peanut butter in wooden bowl; mix well. Spoon into prepared pie plate. Sprinkle with pecans. Freeze for 2 to 3 hours or until firm. May use prepared graham cracker shell.

PECAN PIES

Yield:
12 servings

Approx Per
Serving:
Cal 453
Prot 4 g
Carbo 54 g
T Fat 26 g
50% Calories
from Fat
Chol 53 mg
Fiber 1 g
Sod 310 mg

1 cup sugar
1 cup dark corn syrup
3 eggs, beaten
1/2 cup margarine, chopped
1 1/2 teaspoons vanilla extract
1 cup chopped pecans
2 unbaked (9-inch) pie shells

Combine sugar, corn syrup, eggs, margarine and vanilla in bowl; mix well. Stir in pecans. Spoon into pie shells. Bake at 350 degrees for 30 to 35 minutes or until set.

RHUBARB PIE

Yield:
6 servings

Approx Per
Serving:
Cal 491
Prot 7 g
Carbo 64 g
T Fat 24 g
43% Calories
from Fat
Chol 127 mg
Fiber 2 g
Sod 452 mg

3 egg yolks
1/4 cup butter, softened
3 tablespoons orange juice
1 cup sugar
1/4 cup flour
1/2 teaspoon salt
2 1/2 cups coarsely chopped rhubarb
3 egg whites
1/4 cup sugar
1 unbaked (9-inch) pie shell
1/3 cup chopped pecans

Beat egg yolks in mixer bowl until frothy. Add butter and orange juice; mix well. Beat in 1 cup sugar, flour and salt. Stir in rhubarb. Beat egg whites in mixer bowl until soft peaks form. Add 1/4 cup sugar gradually, beating constantly until stiff peaks form. Fold into rhubarb mixture. Spoon into pie shell; sprinkle with pecans. Place on bottom rack of oven. Bake at 375 degrees for 10 minutes. Reduce temperature to 350 degrees. Bake on middle shelf for 35 to 40 minutes or until set.

OLD FRONTIER VINEGAR PIE

Yield:
8 servings

**Approx Per
Serving:**
*Cal 358
Prot 5 g
Carbo 55 g
T Fat 14 g
35% Calories
from Fat
Chol 87 mg
Fiber 1 g
Sod 286 mg*

6 tablespoons flour
3 tablespoons cornstarch
1 cup sugar
3 cups boiling water
3 egg yolks, slightly
beaten
1/2 cup vinegar

2 tablespoons butter
1/4 teaspoon salt
1 baked (10-inch)
deep-dish pie shell
3 egg whites
6 tablespoons sugar

Combine flour, cornstarch and 1 cup sugar in saucepan; mix well. Stir in boiling water. Cook over low heat for 15 minutes, stirring frequently. Stir a small amount of hot mixture into egg yolks; stir egg yolks into hot mixture. Cook over low heat until thickened, stirring constantly. Remove from heat. Stir in vinegar, butter and salt. Spoon into pie shell. Beat egg whites in mixer bowl until soft peaks form. Add 6 tablespoons sugar gradually, beating constantly until stiff peaks form. Spread over filling, sealing to edge. Bake at 300 degrees for 15 to 20 minutes or until light brown.

QUICK PIE CRUSTS

Yield:
12 servings

**Approx Per
Serving:**
*Cal 156
Prot 2 g
Carbo 16 g
T Fat 10 g
55% Calories
from Fat
Chol 0 mg
Fiber 1 g
Sod 96 mg*

2 cups flour
1/4 teaspoon baking
powder
1/2 teaspoon salt
1/2 cup vegetable oil
1/4 cup water

Combine flour, baking powder and salt in bowl; mix well. Add oil and water, stirring until mixture forms a ball. Shape into 2 balls. Chill, wrapped in plastic wrap, for 30 minutes or longer. Roll each portion to fit pie plate on lightly floured surface. Fit into two 9-inch pie plates. Bake as directed, using your favorite pie recipe.

CHURCH WINDOW CANDY

Yield:
24 servings

Approx Per
Serving:
Cal 127
Prot 1 g
Carbo 11 g
T Fat 10 g
65% Calories
from Fat
Chol 5 mg
Fiber 1 g
Sod 23 mg

1 cup semisweet
  chocolate chips
1/4 cup butter
3 cups multicolored
  miniature
  marshmallows

1³/4 cups chopped pecans

Combine chocolate chips and butter in microwave-safe dish. Microwave on High for 2 to 2¹/2 minutes or until smooth; stir. Stir in marshmallows. Shape into two 1¹/2x6-inch logs. Sprinkle with pecans. Chill, wrapped in waxed paper, until firm. Cut into ¹/2-inch slices.

PERFECT DIVINITY

Yield:
100 servings

Approx Per
Serving:
Cal 61
Prot <1 g
Carbo 13 g
T Fat 1 g
17% Calories
from Fat
Chol 0 mg
Fiber <1 g
Sod 9 mg

5 cups sugar
1 cup light corn syrup
1 cup water
¹/8 teaspoon salt

5 egg whites, stiffly
  beaten
1 teaspoon vanilla extract
1¹/2 cups chopped pecans

Bring sugar, corn syrup, water and salt to a rolling boil over medium-high heat, stirring constantly. Boil, covered, for 2 minutes; remove cover. Cook to 234 degrees on candy thermometer, soft-ball stage. Pour hot mixture gradually over egg whites in mixer bowl. Beat at high speed for 15 minutes or until divinity begins to lose its luster and becomes very stiff. Stir in vanilla and pecans. Spoon onto waxed paper. Let stand until cool. This recipe can be made without considering the weather. May substitute walnuts for pecans.

PERFECT FUDGE

Yield:
36 servings

*Approx Per
Serving:
Cal 125
Prot 2 g
Carbo 16 g
T Fat 7 g
49% Calories
from Fat
Chol 4 mg
Fiber 1 g
Sod 23 mg*

1 (14-ounce) can
  sweetened condensed
  milk
3 cups semisweet
  chocolate chips

1/8 teaspoon salt
1 teaspoon vanilla extract
1 cup chopped pecans

Heat condensed milk in saucepan over medium heat. Stir in chocolate chips. Cook until chocolate melts, stirring frequently. Remove from heat. Stir in salt and vanilla. Add pecans; mix well. Pour into waxed paper-lined dish. Chill for 2 hours or longer. Cut into 1-inch squares. Store loosely at room temperature.

TOFFEE

Yield:
20 servings

*Approx Per
Serving:
Cal 90
Prot 1 g
Carbo 16 g
T Fat 15 g
66% Calories
from Fat
Chol 25 mg
Fiber 1 g
Sod 95 mg*

1 cup sugar
3 tablespoons water
1 cup butter
1 teaspoon rum extract

1 cup miniature
  chocolate chips
3/4 cup chopped pecans

Combine sugar, water and butter in heavy 3- or 4-quart saucepan. Cook over low heat until butter and sugar melt, stirring constantly. Increase heat to medium-high. Cook to 320 degrees on candy thermometer, stirring constantly with wooden spoon. Stir in rum extract. Pour into buttered aluminum 7x11-inch or 9x9-inch pan. Sprinkle with chocolate chips. Let stand until chocolate melts; spread evenly. Sprinkle with pecans. Float pan in sink filled with cold water. Let stand until set. Twist pan; lift candy out of pan. Break into pieces. Do not substitute margarine for butter in this recipe.

NOAH'S ARK BROWNIES

Yield:
42 servings

Approx Per Serving:
Cal 305
Prot 4 g
Carbo 32 g
T Fat 19 g
54% Calories from Fat
Chol 59 mg
Fiber 1 g
Sod 102 mg

2 cups butter
12 (1-ounce) squares
    semisweet chocolate
3 cups minus 6
    tablespoons flour

2¼ teaspoons vanilla
    extract
7 eggs
4 cups sugar
4 cups chopped walnuts

Heat butter and chocolate in saucepan over low heat until melted, stirring frequently. Remove from heat. Stir in flour and vanilla. Beat eggs and sugar in mixer bowl until lemon-colored. Add chocolate mixture. Beat at low speed until blended. Stir in chopped walnuts. Spoon into greased 9x13-inch baking pan and greased 8x8-inch baking pan. Bake at 350 degrees for 35 minutes for large pan and 30 minutes for small pan. Let stand until cool. Cut into bars.

ROCKY ROAD BROWNIES

Yield:
36 servings

Approx Per Serving:
Cal 210
Prot 2 g
Carbo 29 g
T Fat 11 g
44% Calories from Fat
Chol 34 mg
Fiber 1 g
Sod 90 mg

1 cup flour
1 cup sugar
¹/₃ cup baking cocoa
1 cup melted butter
2 eggs
1 teaspoon vanilla extract
1 cup chopped pecans
1 (10-ounce) package
    miniature
    marshmallows

1 (1-pound) package
    confectioners' sugar
¹/₃ cup baking cocoa
¹/₂ cup melted butter
¹/₂ cup evaporated milk
1 teaspoon vanilla extract

Combine flour, sugar and ¹/₃ cup cocoa in bowl; mix well. Stir in 1 cup melted butter. Add eggs 1 at a time, mixing well after each addition. Stir in 1 teaspoon vanilla and pecans. Spoon into greased and floured 9x13-inch baking pan. Bake at 275 degrees for 35 to 40 minutes or until edges pull from sides of pan. Sprinkle with marshmallows. Combine confectioners' sugar and ¹/₃ cup cocoa in bowl; mix well. Stir in ¹/₂ cup melted butter, evaporated milk and 1 teaspoon vanilla. Spread evenly over marshmallow layer while brownies are hot. Let stand until cool. Cut into squares.

GRANDMA'S CHOCOLATE BARS

Yield:
48 servings

Approx Per Serving:
Cal 145
Prot 1 g
Carbo 22 g
T Fat 6 g
39% Calories from Fat
Chol 19 mg
Fiber <1 g
Sod 63 mg

2 cups flour
2 cups sugar
1/2 cup butter
1/2 cup shortening
1 cup strong coffee
1/4 cup baking cocoa
1/2 cup buttermilk
2 eggs, beaten
1 teaspoon baking soda

1 teaspoon vanilla extract
1/2 cup butter
2 tablespoons baking cocoa
1/4 cup milk
31/2 cups confectioners' sugar
1 teaspoon vanilla extract

Combine flour and sugar in bowl; mix well. Combine 1/2 cup butter, shortening, coffee and 1/4 cup cocoa in saucepan. Bring to a boil, stirring constantly. Pour over flour mixture. Cool slightly. Stir in buttermilk, eggs, baking soda and 1 teaspoon vanilla. Spoon into buttered 11x17-inch baking pan. Bake at 400 degrees for 20 minutes or until brownies test done. Combine 1/2 cup butter, 2 tablespoons cocoa and milk in saucepan. Bring to a boil, stirring constantly. Remove from heat. Stir in confectioners' sugar and vanilla. Spread over hot brownies. Let stand until cool. Cut into bars.

CHOCOLATE CHERRY BARS

Yield:
36 servings

Approx Per Serving:
Cal 144
Prot 2 g
Carbo 25 g
T Fat 5 g
29% Calories from Fat
Chol 12 mg
Fiber <1 g
Sod 149 mg

1 (2-layer) package devil's food cake mix
1 (21-ounce) can cherry pie filling
1 teaspoon almond extract
2 eggs, beaten

1 cup sugar
5 tablespoons margarine
1/3 cup milk
1 cup semisweet chocolate chips

Combine cake mix, pie filling, almond extract and eggs in bowl; mix well. Spoon into greased and floured 9x13-inch baking pan. Bake at 350 degrees for 25 to 30 minutes or until edges pull from sides of pan. Bring sugar, margarine and milk to a boil in saucepan, stirring constantly. Boil for 1 minute, stirring constantly. Stir in chocolate chips until smooth. Spread over hot baked layer. Let stand until cool. Cut into bars.

CHOCOLATE-COVERED CHERRY COOKIES

Yield:
18 servings

Approx Per
Serving:
Cal 227
Prot 3 g
Carbo 36 g
T Fat 9 g
35% Calories
from Fat
Chol 15 mg
Fiber 2 g
Sod 121 mg

1 (10-ounce) jar maraschino cherries
1 1/2 cups flour
1/2 cup baking cocoa
1/4 teaspoon each salt, baking powder and baking soda
1/2 cup margarine, softened
1 cup sugar
1 egg, beaten
1 1/2 teaspoons vanilla extract
1 cup semisweet chocolate chips
1/2 cup sweetened condensed milk

Drain maraschino cherries, reserving juice. Mix flour, cocoa, salt, baking powder and baking soda in bowl. Beat margarine and sugar in mixer bowl until light. Add egg and vanilla, beating until smooth. Add dry ingredients gradually, beating until blended. Shape into 1-inch balls; place on ungreased cookie sheet. Make indention in center of each ball with thumb. Place maraschino cherry in indention. Combine chocolate chips and condensed milk in saucepan. Cook until chocolate melts, stirring constantly. Stir in 4 teaspoons reserved cherry juice. Spoon 1 teaspoon frosting over each cherry. Bake at 350 degrees for 10 minutes. Remove to wire rack to cool.

CHOCOLATE CHIP COOKIES

Yield:
36 servings

Approx Per
Serving:
Cal 132
Prot 1 g
Carbo 15 g
T Fat 8 g
54% Calories
from Fat
Chol 6 mg
Fiber 1 g
Sod 82 mg

3/4 cup butter-flavored shortening
1 1/4 cups packed brown sugar
2 tablespoons milk
1 tablespoon vanilla extract
1 egg
1 3/4 cups flour
1 teaspoon salt
3/4 teaspoon baking soda
1 cup semisweet chocolate chips
1 cup pecan pieces

Cream shortening, brown sugar, milk and vanilla in mixer bowl until light and fluffy. Beat in egg until smooth. Add mixture of flour, salt and baking soda gradually; mix well. Stir in chocolate chips and pecans. Drop by rounded tablespoonfuls 3 inches apart onto ungreased cookie sheet. Bake at 375 degrees for 8 minutes for chewy cookies or for 11 minutes for crisp cookies. Cool on cookie sheet for 2 minutes. Remove to wire rack to cool completely.

CREAM CHEESE COOKIES

Yield:
30 servings

*Approx Per
Serving:*
Cal 162
Prot 2 g
Carbo 14 g
T Fat 12 g
*63% Calories
from Fat*
Chol 25 mg
Fiber <1 g
Sod 191 mg

8 ounces cream cheese,
    softened
1 cup butter, softened
1 cup sugar

1¹/₂ teaspoons vanilla
    extract
2 cups self-rising flour
1 cup chopped pecans

Beat cream cheese, butter, sugar and vanilla in mixer bowl until light and fluffy. Add flour, stirring until blended. Stir in pecans. Drop by teaspoonfuls onto ungreased cookie sheet. Bake at 350 degrees for 15 minutes or until edges are brown. Remove to wire rack to cool.

CRUNCHY COOKIES

Yield:
24 servings

*Approx Per
Serving:*
Cal 180
Prot 2 g
Carbo 19 g
T Fat 11 g
*55% Calories
from Fat*
Chol 21 mg
Fiber 1 g
Sod 193 mg

1 (16-ounce) package
    graham crackers
1 cup butter

¹/₂ cup sugar
¹/₂ cup crushed pecans

Line bottom of cookie sheet with graham crackers. Bring butter and sugar to a boil in saucepan, stirring constantly. Boil for 1 minute, stirring constantly. Stir in pecans. Pour over graham crackers. Bake at 350 degrees for 10 minutes.

Fruit Bars

Yield:
35 servings

Approx Per Serving:
Cal 88
Prot 1 g
Carbo 13 g
T Fat 4 g
39% Calories from Fat
Chol 12 mg
Fiber 1 g
Sod 65 mg

1 cup self-rising flour
1¹/₄ cups sugar
¹/₄ cup melted margarine
2 eggs, beaten

1 cup chopped pecans
1 cup dried apricots, sliced or chopped

Sift flour and sugar in bowl; mix well. Stir in margarine, eggs, pecans and apricots in order listed. Spread in non-stick 9x13-inch baking pan. Bake at 350 degrees for 25 to 30 minutes or until brown. Bake at 375 degrees for 20 to 25 minutes for chewy bars. Cool in pan. Cut into 2x2-inch bars. May substitute dates, figs, prunes or any combination of dried fruit for apricots.

Ginger Cookies

Yield:
48 servings

Approx Per Serving:
Cal 150
Prot 1 g
Carbo 23 g
T Fat 6 g
36% Calories from Fat
Chol 24 mg
Fiber <1 g
Sod 176 mg

1 teaspoon salt
4 cups flour
4 teaspoons baking soda
1 tablespoon ginger
2 teaspoons cinnamon
2 teaspoons ground cloves

1 teaspoon nutmeg
1¹/₂ cups butter
2 cups sugar
¹/₂ cup molasses
2 eggs, beaten
1 cup sugar

Sift salt, flour, baking soda, ginger, cinnamon, cloves and nutmeg together. Cream butter in mixer bowl until light and fluffy. Add 2 cups sugar, molasses and eggs, beating until smooth. Add dry ingredients; mix well. Shape by rounded teaspoonfuls into balls; roll in 1 cup sugar. Place on ungreased cookie sheet; flatten with fork. Bake at 350 degrees for 12 to 15 minutes or until brown. Remove to wire rack to cool.

MAGIC COOKIE BARS

Yield:
24 servings

Approx Per
Serving:
Cal 200
Prot 3 g
Carbo 22 g
T Fat 12 g
53% Calories
from Fat
Chol 16 mg
Fiber 1 g
Sod 107 mg

1/2 cup butter
11/2 cups graham
cracker crumbs
1 (14-ounce) can
sweetened condensed
milk

1 cup semisweet
chocolate chips
1 (3-ounce) can flaked
coconut
1 cup chopped walnuts

Melt butter in 9x13-inch baking pan, tilting pan to coat. Layer graham cracker crumbs, condensed milk, chocolate chips, coconut and walnuts in order listed over butter; press gently. Bake at 350 degrees for 25 to 30 minutes or until light brown. Cut into bars when cool. Store, loosely covered, at room temperature.

MEXICAN YULETIDE COOKIES

Yield:
78 servings

Approx Per
Serving:
Cal 57
Prot 1 g
Carbo 6 g
T Fat 4 g
55% Calories
from Fat
Chol 9 mg
Fiber <1 g
Sod 28 mg

1 cup butter, softened
3/4 cup confectioners'
sugar
1 egg
11/2 teaspoons vanilla
extract

1/8 teaspoon salt
2 cups sifted flour
1 cup rolled oats
1 cup chopped pecans
1 cup confectioners'
sugar

Cream butter in mixer bowl until light and fluffy. Add 3/4 cup confectioners' sugar, beating until smooth. Beat in egg and vanilla until blended. Stir in salt, flour, oats and pecans. Shape by rounded teaspoonfuls into balls. Place on ungreased cookie sheet. Bake at 325 degrees for 20 minutes. Roll warm cookies in 1 cup confectioners' sugar. Cool on wire rack.

TWO HUNDRED FIFTY-DOLLAR COOKIES

Yield:
112 servings

Approx Per Serving:
Cal 149
Prot 2 g
Carbo 18 g
T Fat 8 g
48% Calories from Fat
Chol 17 mg
Fiber 1 g
Sod 79 mg

5 cups rolled oats
2 cups butter, softened
2 cups packed brown sugar
2 cups sugar
4 eggs
2 teaspoons vanilla extract
4 cups flour

1 teaspoon salt
2 teaspoons baking powder
2 teaspoons baking soda
4 cups semisweet chocolate chips
1 (8-ounce) chocolate candy bar, grated
3 cups chopped pecans

Process oats in blender until finely ground. Cream butter, brown sugar and sugar in mixer bowl until light and fluffy. Beat in eggs and vanilla. Add oats, flour, salt, baking powder and baking soda; mix well. Stir in chocolate chips, grated candy bar and pecans. Chill for 30 minutes. Shape dough into balls. Place 2 inches apart on cookie sheet. Bake at 375 degrees for 6 minutes. Remove to wire rack to cool.

OATMEAL SQUARES

Yield:
36 servings

Approx Per Serving:
Cal 95
Prot 1 g
Carbo 16 g
T Fat 3 g
28% Calories from Fat
Chol 19 mg
Fiber <1 g
Sod 84 mg

1 1/4 cups hot water
1 cup rolled oats
1/2 cup butter, softened
1 cup sugar
1 cup packed brown sugar

2 eggs
1 1/2 cups flour
1 teaspoon baking soda
1 teaspoon cinnamon
1/2 teaspoon salt

Pour hot water over oats in bowl. Cream butter, sugar and brown sugar in mixer bowl until light and fluffy. Beat in eggs until blended. Add flour, baking soda, cinnamon and salt; mix well. Stir in oat mixture. Spread in greased 9x13-inch baking pan. Bake at 350 degrees for 35 minutes. Cool. Cut into squares.

FRUITED SHORTBREAD COOKIES

Yield:
36 servings

Approx Per Serving:
Cal 109
Prot 1 g
Carbo 14 g
T Fat 6 g
45% Calories from Fat
Chol 6 mg
Fiber <1 g
Sod 91 mg

1 cup margarine, softened
1¹/₂ cups confectioners' sugar
1 egg
1 (9-ounce) package mincemeat, crumbled
1 teaspoon vanilla extract
2¹/₂ cups flour
1 teaspoon baking soda
1 teaspoon cream of tartar

Beat margarine and confectioners' sugar in mixer bowl until light and fluffy. Beat in egg until blended. Add mincemeat and vanilla; mix well. Stir in mixture of flour, baking soda and cream of tartar. Shape into 1¹/₄-inch balls. Place on ungreased cookie sheet; flatten slightly. Bake at 375 degrees for 10 to 12 minutes or until light brown. Remove to wire rack to cool. May frost cookies with your favorite icing.

SNOWBALLS

Yield:
66 servings

Approx Per Serving:
Cal 97
Prot 1 g
Carbo 10 g
T Fat 6 g
56% Calories from Fat
Chol 9 mg
Fiber <1 g
Sod 34 mg

1 cup butter, softened
¹/₂ cup sugar
1 teaspoon vanilla extract
2 cups flour
1 cup chopped pecans
1 (16-ounce) package chocolate kisses
³/₄ cup confectioners' sugar

Cream butter, sugar and vanilla in mixer bowl until light and fluffy. Stir in flour and pecans. Knead until creamy. Shape 1 teaspoon of dough around each chocolate kiss, enclosing completely. Roll to form a ball. Place on cookie sheet. Bake at 375 degrees for 12 minutes. Remove to wire rack to cool. Dust with confectioners' sugar.

SUGAR COOKIES

Yield:
48 servings

Approx Per
Serving:
Cal 80
Prot 1 g
Carbo 10 g
T Fat 4 g
47% Calories
from Fat
Chol 10 mg
Fiber <1 g
Sod 22 mg

$^1/_2$ cup shortening
$^1/_2$ cup butter, softened
1 cup sugar
1 egg

$^1/_4$ cup sour milk
$2^3/_4$ cups flour
1 teaspoon vanilla extract

Cream shortening and butter in mixer bowl until light and fluffy. Add sugar, beating until smooth. Stir in egg. Add sour milk, flour and vanilla; mix well. Roll dough on floured surface; cut with cookie cutter. Place on cookie sheet. Bake at 350 degrees for 10 to 12 minutes or until brown. Remove to wire rack to cool.

EASY SUGAR COOKIES

Yield:
96 servings

Approx Per
Serving:
Cal 81
Prot 1 g
Carbo 10 g
T Fat 4 g
48% Calories
from Fat
Chol 10 mg
Fiber <1 g
Sod 52 mg

1 cup butter, softened
1 cup confectioners'
  sugar
2 eggs
1 teaspoon cream of
  tartar
1 cup vegetable oil

1 teaspoon baking soda
1 teaspoon salt
$^3/_4$ cup sugar
1 teaspoon vanilla extract
4 cups flour
$1^1/_2$ cups sugar

Beat butter, confectioners' sugar, eggs, cream of tartar, oil, baking soda, salt, $^3/_4$ cup sugar and vanilla in mixer bowl until smooth and creamy. Stir in flour until blended. Chill, covered, overnight. Shape dough into balls; roll in $1^1/_2$ cups sugar. Place on cookie sheet; flatten with glass. Bake at 350 degrees for 12 minutes. Remove to wire rack to cool.

Herbs and Spices

Use fresh whole herbs when possible. When fresh herbs are not available, use whole dried herbs that can be crushed just while adding. Add ground spices toward the end of the cooking time to retain maximum flavor. Whole spices may be added at the beginning but should have a small amount of additional spices added near the end of cooking time also. Store herbs and spices in airtight containers away from the heat of the stove.

Allspice	Pungent aromatic spice, whole or in powdered form. It is excellent in marinades, particularly in game marinade, or in curries.
Basil	Can be chopped and added to cold poultry salads. If the recipe calls for tomatoes or tomato sauce, add a touch of basil to bring out a rich flavor.
Chervil	One of the traditional *fines herbes* used in French cooking. (The others are tarragon, parsley and chives.) It is good in omelets and soups.
Cinnamon	Ground from the bark of the cinnamon tree, it is delicious in desserts as well as savory dishes.
Coriander	Seeds used whole or ground, this slightly lemony spice adds an unusual flavor to soups, stews, chili dishes, curries and desserts.
Cumin	A staple spice in Mexican cooking. Use in meat, rice, cheese, egg and fish dishes.
Ginger	The whole root used fresh, dried or ground is a sweet, pungent addition to desserts or oriental-style dishes.
Marjoram	An aromatic herb of the mint family, it is good in soups, sauces, stuffings and stews.
Mint	Use fresh, dried or ground with vegetables, desserts, fruits, jelly, lamb or tea. Fresh sprigs of mint make attractive aromatic garnishes.
Nutmeg	Use the whole spice or a bit of freshly ground for flavor in beverages, breads and desserts. A sprinkle on top is both a flavor enhancer and an attractive garnish.
Oregano	A staple, savory herb in Italian, Spanish, Greek and Mexican cuisines. It is very good in dishes with a tomato foundation, especially in combination with basil.
Rosemary	This pungent herb is especially good in poultry and fish dishes and in such accompaniments as stuffings.
Sage	This herb is a perennial favorite with all kinds of poultry and stuffings.
Tarragon	One of the *fines herbes*. Goes well with all poultry dishes whether hot or cold.
Thyme	Usually used in combination with bay leaf in soups, stews and sauces.
Turmeric	Ground from a root related to ginger, this is an essential in curry powder. Also used in pickles, relishes, cheese and egg dishes.

Do You Know What It Means?

Bard	To cover lean meats with bacon or pork fat before cooking in order to prevent dryness.
Blanch	To immerse, usually vegetables or fruit, briefly into boiling water to inactivate enzymes, loosen skin, or soak away excess salt.
Braise	To cook, especially meats, covered, in a small amount of liquid.
Caramelize	To melt sugar in a heavy pan over low heat until golden, stirring constantly.
Clarify	To remove impurities from melted butter or margarine by allowing the sediment to settle, then pouring off clear yellow liquid. Other fats may be clarified by straining.
Curdle	To congeal milk with rennet or heat it until solid lumps or curds are formed.
Decant	To pour a liquid such as wine or melted butter carefully from 1 container into another leaving the sediment in the original container.
Deglaze	To heat stock, wine or other liquid in the pan in which meat has been cooked, mixing with pan juices and sediment to form a gravy or sauce base.
Degorger	To remove strong flavors or impurities before cooking, i.e. soaking ham in cold water or sprinkling vegetables with salt, then letting stand for a period of time and pressing out excess fluid.
Degrease	To remove accumulated fat from surface of hot liquids.
Dredge	To coat completely with flour, bread crumbs, etc.
Flambé	To pour warmed Brandy or other spirits over food in a pan, then ignite and continue cooking briefly.
Garnish	To decorate food before serving.
Gratiné	To top a sauced dish with crumbs, cheese or butter, then brown under a broiler.
Julienne	To cut vegetables, fruit, etc. into long thin strips.
Plank	To broil and serve on a board or wooden platter.
Poach	To cook in a small amount of gently simmering liquid.
Purée	To reduce the pulp of cooked fruit and vegetables to a smooth and thick liquid by straining or blending.
Shirr	To crack eggs into individual buttered baking dishes, then bake or broil until whites are set. Chopped meats or vegetables, cheese, cream or bread crumbs may also be added.
Skim	To ladle or spoon off excess fat or scum from the surface of a liquid.
Truss	To bind poultry legs and wings close to the body before cooking.

Substitution Chart

	Instead of	Use
Baking	1 teaspoon baking powder 1 tablespoon cornstarch (for thickening) 1 cup sifted all-purpose flour 1 cup sifted cake flour	$1/4$ teaspoon soda plus $1/2$ teaspoon cream of tartar 2 tablespoons flour or 1 tablespoon tapioca 1 cup plus 2 tablespoons sifted cake flour 1 cup minus 2 tablespoons sifted all-purpose flour
	1 cup dry bread crumbs	$3/4$ cup cracker crumbs
Dairy	1 cup buttermilk 1 cup heavy cream 1 cup light cream 1 cup sour cream 1 cup sour milk	1 cup sour milk or 1 cup yogurt $3/4$ cup skim milk plus $1/3$ cup butter $7/8$ cup skim milk plus 3 tablespoons butter $7/8$ cup sour milk plus 3 tablespoons butter 1 cup milk plus 1 tablespoon vinegar or lemon juice or 1 cup buttermilk
Seasoning	1 teaspoon allspice 1 cup catsup 1 clove of garlic 1 teaspoon Italian spice 1 teaspoon lemon juice 1 tablespoon mustard 1 medium onion	$1/2$ teaspoon cinnamon plus $1/8$ teaspoon cloves 1 cup tomato sauce plus $1/2$ cup sugar plus 2 tablespoons vinegar $1/8$ teaspoon garlic powder or $1/8$ teaspoon instant minced garlic or $3/4$ teaspoon garlic salt or 5 drops of liquid garlic $1/4$ teaspoon each oregano, basil, thyme, rosemary plus dash of cayenne $1/2$ teaspoon vinegar 1 teaspoon dry mustard 1 tablespoon dried minced onion or 1 teaspoon onion powder
Sweet	1 1-ounce square chocolate $1^2/3$ ounces semisweet chocolate 1 cup honey 1 cup granulated sugar	$1/4$ cup cocoa plus 1 teaspoon shortening 1 ounce unsweetened chocolate plus 4 teaspoons granulated sugar 1 to $1^1/4$ cups sugar plus $1/4$ cup liquid or 1 cup corn syrup or molasses 1 cup packed brown sugar or 1 cup corn syrup, molasses or honey minus $1/4$ cup liquid

Index

Mail Order Form

Atlanta's Treasures Cookbook

Telephone Pioneers of America
AT&T, Chapter Office
1200 Peachtree Street
Prom I, Floc 9133
Atlanta, Georgia 30309

Name _____

Address _____

City/State/Zip_____

Number of copies   _____

x Cost ($10.95 per book)   _____

+ Shipping and handling ($2.50 per book)   _____

Total   _____

Make check payable to: Telephone Pioneers of America

Mail Order Form

Atlanta's Treasures Cookbook

Telephone Pioneers of America
AT&T, Chapter Office
1200 Peachtree Street
Prom I, Floc 9133
Atlanta, Georgia 30309

Name _____

Address _____

City/State/Zip_____

Number of copies   _____

x Cost ($10.95 per book)   _____

+ Shipping and handling ($2.50 per book)   _____

Total   _____

Make check payable to: Telephone Pioneers of America

The Swan House - Atlanta Historical Society